WHAT IS
WRONG WITH
THE WORLD?

WHAT IS WRONG WITH THE WORLD?

The Surprising, Hopeful Answer
to the Question We Cannot Avoid

TIMOTHY KELLER

ZONDERVAN
BOOKS

ZONDERVAN BOOKS

What Is Wrong with the World?
Copyright © 2025 by River Road Stewardship LLC

Published by Zondervan, 3950 Sparks Drive SE, Suite 101, Grand Rapids, MI 49546, USA. Zondervan is a registered trademark of The Zondervan Corporation, L.L.C., a wholly owned subsidiary of HarperCollins Christian Publishing, Inc.

Requests for information should be addressed to customercare@harpercollins.com.

Zondervan titles may be purchased in bulk for educational, business, fundraising, or sales promotional use. For information, please email SpecialMarkets@Zondervan.com.

ISBN 978-0-310-37019-2 (audio)

Library of Congress Cataloging-in-Publication Data

Names: Keller, Timothy, 1950–2023 author
Title: What is wrong with the world? : the surprising, hopeful answer to the question we cannot avoid / Timothy Keller.
Description: Grand Rapids, Michigan : Zondervan Books, [2025]
Identifiers: LCCN 2025013230 (print) | LCCN 2025013231 (ebook) | ISBN 9780310370161 hardcover | ISBN 9780310370178 ebook
Subjects: LCSH: Sin—Christianity | Hope—Religious aspects—Christianity
Classification: LCC BT715 .K354 2025 (print) | LCC BT715 (ebook) | DDC 241/.3—dc23 /eng/20250604
LC record available at https://lccn.loc.gov/2025013230
LC ebook record available at https://lccn.loc.gov/2025013231

HarperCollins Publishers, Macken House, 39/40 Mayor Street Upper, Dublin 1, D01 C9W8, Ireland (https://www.harpercollins.com)

Cover illustration: Yuliia Makova / Shutterstock
Interior design: Kristen Sasamoto

Printed in the United States of America

25 26 27 28 29 LBC 5 4 3 2 1

CONTENTS

CONTENTS

PREFACE

Tim preached the sermons on which this book is based in the 1990s as a series under the title "The Faces of Sin." He had preached some of the sermons individually at other times and places, but having a series that examined sin in its many forms and dimensions was important in a place like New York City.

People didn't like the word.

Once after a service a well-dressed woman came up to Tim and shouted angrily (presumably because of the confession of sin in the liturgy of the worship service), "Neither I nor any of my children will ever confess to being sinners!" She then spun on her heel and marched out of the auditorium.

On another occasion, a new convert invited Tim to meet with several of her friends. Their conversation was cordial until one of the women fixed Tim with a hard stare and said, "You think I'm a sinner, don't you?" Tim tried to explain that he did not believe she was different from anyone else. We are *all* sinners who fall short of what God meant us to be; we are all broken, all in need of grace.

It didn't make any difference. The conversation was over. She believed sin was a "nuclear" word, reserved for the scum of the earth, applicable only to murderers, rapists, Nazis, and members of the KKK. Nothing Tim said could convince her otherwise.

The need to explain sin in its many dimensions and its universal contagion of all people is clearly necessary. It's not a concept most people are familiar with, and when they do hear it, there is often resistance. The idea that we have all rebelled, in our own individual ways, against the rightful king of the universe, rejected his love, trampled on his heart . . . well, it just doesn't fit in our good/bad, right/wrong, I'm in/you're out world.

Once, Tim was sharing the gospel with a number of people who lived near our first church in Virginia. One woman had gladly heard the gospel, but when Tim made a second, follow-up visit, he found her sister there, waiting for him.

"You mean to tell me," the sister said with an incredulous sneer, "that some axe murderer who repented and accepted

Jesus would go to heaven and I, who have led a good life without any religion, would not?" Tim agreed that that was indeed the case. The sister fell silent, stunned by his response. Determined to avoid further awkwardness, Tim quickly arranged to meet the first woman—the one who had initially welcomed the message—on another day. (The ink was barely dry on his ordination papers at that point, and he had not yet encountered that kind of pushback. He got better as time went by.)

In the years since Tim died, I have tried to bring some kind of order to all the books, papers, talks, sermons, lectures, classes, notes, journals, and jottings he left behind. This has not been easy: If an idea struck him and there was no paper at hand, he was just as likely to write down his thought on the inside cover of whatever book he was holding. (And he never went anywhere without a book, even when he took out the trash to the other end of the hall where the refuse chute was located!) Additionally, his computer held around sixty thousand files, and it has been intimidating to make sense of those because of his file-naming system. If he was writing a sermon or a book, each revision or significant editorial change was treated as a new document and given its own name according to a shorthand that made sense to him. So I might encounter a file named "FOS-1.1. 02/96," which

I think might be read as "Faces of Sin, version 1.1, written February 2, 1996." Maybe.

I felt on surer ground dealing with the papers in the sixteen file drawers, although they were packed so tightly in each drawer (as well as boxes and cupboards) that pulling out one file folder was an exercise in itself, and putting it back defeated even weight-lifting gym rats.

I did, however, manage to extract the folder titled "The Faces of Sin" and, after consulting with a number of knowledgeable people, decided it would be a good start for a book about sin. Since I have been Tim's oral-to-written-style editor for most of his books, this seemed like it would be an easy task, but of course nothing is as easy as we hope it will be. Thanks are due to David McCormick, our agent for many years who is now a friend and advocate as well; to Webster Younce, a former elder at Redeemer who is now vice president and executive editor at Zondervan/HarperCollins; and especially to Braedon Gregg, who did the developmental editing and has helped turn some of Tim's works from oral to written form. He has a great feel for Tim's voice, and I couldn't have done it without him.

Each chapter ends with a prayer because Tim was aware, as all mature Christians are, that we deceive ourselves most concerning our own sinfulness. We treat people harshly and call it "straight talking," or skip private or corporate communion with God and call it "self-care." You can't confess something that you have convinced yourself you aren't guilty of. So as you read, allow God to probe you for your hidden sins and to give you a contrite and broken heart over the ways you have broken both his law and his heart. Grace is there for the asking.

Kathy Keller

INTRODUCTION

Questions arise in our minds and hearts every day. Some are easy to answer: "What should I wear today?" or "What should I make for dinner?" Some are weightier and harder to determine: "Should I move to a different city?" or "Should I marry this person?" But one question rises above all others, the supreme question that each of us asks ourselves time and time again: *What is wrong with the world? What is wrong with the human race?*

That question can take other forms: Why do we treat each other so terribly? Why do we do such horrible things, such as genocide and murder and driving others into poverty? Why can we not live at peace with one another and just be happy? Whatever form it takes, this question is central to making sense of existence.

Years ago I read a book on the subject of evil in modern life and how we view it.[1] In his introduction, the author noted that it was rare for a week to pass without him seeing news reports detailing horrific events. He noted an account of teenagers performing contract killings for just a few dollars, a story of a man shot in the head over the keys to a car, and—the week he finished the book—reports of atrocities in concentration camps where ethnic cleansing was happening.[2]

What's wrong with us? What could lead human beings to do things like this? If you don't ask that question—if that question doesn't burn in your heart—your head is in the sand.

Many attempts have been made at answering this question. Some people hear news of ethnic cleansing and point to a sociological reason, arguing that it's clearly the result of racism. But that response doesn't actually answer the question. *Why* are we humans capable of such racist atrocities? How can we be so callous toward another race in the first place? Others may read the story about teenagers turned hit men and turn to sociology as well, saying it's the result of poverty. But why would a human being respond to poverty with murder, of all things?

The sociological factor is not, at root, the answer. Sociological reasons may be the *occasion* for murder, but they are not the cause. The answer the Bible gives us for why we do such heinous things is both simple and complex. That answer is sin. Many reading this may be irritated and think this is a primitive and old-fashioned analysis. My response—and the Bible's—is yes! Of course it's primitive and old-fashioned—because it's true and deeply woven into the world and its entire history. It would be a terrible answer if it *weren't* old-fashioned.

But—and this is where the complexity of the answer begins to appear—sin is not limited to the most grievous things we read about in the news. The questions we ask about humanity's depravity, questions prompted by the previous stories, also extend to our own selves. How does it become so easy for us to lie to someone? Why do we keep coming back to crippling addictions instead of giving them up the instant we realize they're hurting us?

The truth of the matter is that we will *never* be able to answer these questions unless we come to understand sin. We will never be able to resolve our personal problems, let alone the rest of the world's problems, unless we possess a full comprehension of sin. After all, how can we prescribe a remedy unless we first diagnose the disease?

When many of us hear the word *sin*, we think about the didactic parts of Scripture where sin is *taught about*—the Ten Commandments, the specifications of God's law, the thou shalt nots, and so on. That is true so far as it goes. But the Bible's depiction of sin is much more comprehensive than just what is contained in those passages. The Bible gives us many concrete examples and metaphors to show us the full range of what sin is, how it affects us, and, yes, why we keep coming back to it. In Genesis sin is depicted as a wild beast in the story of Cain. In 2 Kings, we see sin as leprosy in the story of Naaman. In the gospel of Mark, Jesus uses the metaphor of sin as leaven when he reprimands the Pharisees. In addition, the Bible speaks of sin as self-deception, self-righteousness, and slavery. This book addresses each of these metaphors and what it means for our understanding of what is wrong with the world. Each chapter in the book illuminates a specific aspect of sin and explores how we might be saved from it.

Some readers may be thinking, "Why spend an entire book talking about such a negative and unpopular subject as sin?" Others of you might not even be sure what you think about Christianity. "I don't know if I believe in God," you may say. "Why on earth would I be interested in hearing about sin?"

I'll give you two reasons why it is not just important but *all-important* that you understand sin. The first reason is that the biblical teaching about sin is one of the strongest arguments for the truth of Christianity. The second is that it equips you to best handle life as it is.

To take the first reason, I can show you person after person (and I'll mention some of them as the book goes on) who abandoned Christianity but were pushed back to embrace it because nothing other than the idea of sin could account for the darkest depths of human behavior. These individuals saw human evil up close. The Bible was the only way they could find to explain what they saw.

In *The Death of Satan: How Americans Have Lost the Sense of Evil*, Andrew Delbanco, a professor of American studies at Columbia University and a self-described secular liberal, argues that if you get rid of the ideas of religion along with the moral, spiritual idea of sin, you are forced to conclude that the reason we do the terrible things to each other as described earlier is due to either biology, psychology, or sociology. That creates all sorts of problems. As Delbanco writes, "A gulf has opened up in our culture between the visibility of evil and the intellectual resources available for coping with it."[3]

If the terrible acts humans commit are a result of biology, they're part of our evolutionary makeup, where aggression is bound up with the idea of the survival of the fittest. Or the reasons are found in psychology: We do these terrible things because of repressed emotions. Or in sociology, we do them because of economic deprivation. But when you get a close-up view of the horrors of evil, all those theories fall apart. If those theories are true, then we really can't help doing what we do and therefore we're not really evil. But anyone who witnesses a parent killing their child knows that makes no sense. These acts can't be so easily explained away, no matter how hard we try. As the serial killer Hannibal Lecter says to the FBI agent trying to analyze him in *The Silence of the Lambs*, "Nothing happened to me, Officer Starling. *I* happened. You can't reduce me to a set of influences. You've given up good and evil for behaviorism . . . You've got everybody in moral-dignity pants—nothing is ever anybody's fault. Look at me, Officer Starling. Can you stand to say I'm evil ?"[4]

In his book *The Brothers Karamazov*, Russian novelist Fyodor Dostoevsky addresses the idea of seeing biology as the culprit: "People talk sometimes of a bestial cruelty, but that's a great injustice and insult to the beasts; a beast can never be so cruel as a man, so artistically cruel. The tiger only tears and gnaws, that's all he can do. He would never think of nailing people by the ears, even if he were able to do it."[5] As Dostoevsky knew, something else is going on here, something beyond biology or sociology or psychology. That something is sin.

The second reason it's all-important to understand sin is that if you *don't* take up the old-fashioned, traditional understanding of it, you will be led into countless personal and social miscalculations. You will not be able to deal with life as it is. Not only that, but you won't be able to understand the glory of God's love and grace. You'll never be stunned or amazed by it.

Here is what I mean. If someone came up to you and said, "I was at your house the other day and you weren't there. Then a man came with a bill for you, and I paid it," how would you react? Well, it depends on the size of the bill, doesn't it?

What if it was postage due for seventy-five cents? That's one thing. What if it was the landlord demanding rent? That's another thing. What if it was an auditor from the IRS saying, "You owe ten years of back taxes, and we're repossessing your property unless you pay up"? That's something else entirely. Until you know whether the bill was $10 or $1,000 or $100,000, you don't know whether you've been helped a little or utterly saved. You don't know whether to shake the person's hand or kiss their feet and swear eternal loyalty.

How does this relate to the idea of sin? Here's how. If there is a lack of joy in your life today, if the thought of Jesus dying for you does not transfix and transform you, if you're not able to draw power out of the thought of what he has done for you on the cross, then you don't understand the enormity and power of your sin. You haven't really seen how much of a debt Christ paid for you. You don't know how far he has brought you. You don't know the magnitude of what he has done. And you don't know the seriousness and depth of your sin that led him to do what he did.

Put another way, if you don't understand sin, you are neither pessimistic enough nor optimistic enough to deal with life. On the one hand, if you believe the reason people do the terrible things they do is because of poor social conditioning or evolution or repressed psychology, you'll never be able to deal with life as it is. You'll be like Agent Starling, speechless before Hannibal Lecter. You won't be pessimistic enough, so to speak, to grapple with the bleak realities of life.

In her book *Creed or Chaos?*, English author Dorothy L. Sayers observes that Christianity, far from its caricature as an escape from reality, is a supremely clear-eyed way of viewing the world. She writes, "It seems to me quite disastrous that the idea should have got about that Christianity is an other-worldly, unreal, idealistic kind of religion that suggests that if we are good we shall be happy. On the contrary, it is fiercely and even harshly realistic, insisting that there are certain eternal achievements that make even happiness look like trash."[6] In other words, one of the things that precludes an "unreal, idealistic" view of life is Christianity's clear-eyed view of sin.

On the other hand, without a full understanding of sin, you won't have the grounds for the optimism necessary to remain hopeful in the midst of life's harsh realities. Only via a clear view of sin can you see there are some things Jesus has done *for* us and has given *to* us and can do *in* us and *is* doing in us that make any earthly happiness look like little but trash. That's what provides the joy and the confidence to survive. If you don't understand sin, you'll be neither pessimistic enough nor optimistic enough to deal with life.

If we stand any chance of answering the question of what is wrong with the world—much less of being saved from the answer to that question—we must begin with understanding the complexity and multifaceted nature of sin and end with understanding the unfailing love of a God who chooses to save us from it. This book will show you how.

CHAPTER 1

SIN AS PREDATOR

Genesis 4:3–15

[3] In the course of time Cain brought some of the fruits of the soil as an offering to the LORD. [4] But Abel brought fat portions from some of the firstborn of his flock. The LORD looked with favor on Abel and his offering, [5] but on Cain and his offering he did not look with favor. So Cain was very angry, and his face was downcast.

[6] Then the LORD said to Cain, "Why are you angry? Why is your face downcast? [7] If you do what is right, will you not be accepted? But if you do not do

what is right, sin is crouching at your door; it desires to have you, but you must master it."

8 Now Cain said to his brother Abel, "Let's go out to the field." And while they were in the field, Cain attacked his brother Abel and killed him.

9 Then the LORD said to Cain, "Where is your brother Abel?"

"I don't know," he replied. "Am I my brother's keeper?"

10 The LORD said, "What have you done? Listen! Your brother's blood cries out to me from the ground. 11 Now you are under a curse and driven from the ground, which opened its mouth to receive your brother's blood from your hand. 12 When you work the ground, it will no longer yield its crops for you. You will be a restless wanderer on the earth."

13 Cain said to the LORD, "My punishment is more than I can bear. 14 Today you are driving me from the land, and I will be hidden from your presence; I will be a restless wanderer on the earth, and whoever finds me will kill me."

15 But the LORD said to him, "Not so; if anyone kills Cain, he will suffer vengeance seven times over." Then the LORD put a mark on Cain so that no one who found him would kill him.

Years ago I watched the first *Terminator* movie with one of my sons. The film is a violent but well-made work of science fiction about a futuristic cyborg sent back in time to assassinate the protagonist, Sarah Connor. It wasn't until I rewatched it that I realized how much of Sarah's predicament is created solely by people underestimating the predatory power of the killer pursuing her.

Everyone in the film continually fails to understand the power of the Terminator. He *looks* like a human being, but he is actually a nearly indestructible machine. Early in the film, a police lieutenant tells Sarah, who in fear has telephoned the police station from a bar, "You're in a public place, so you'll be safe till we get there."[1] The lieutenant believes that no one would possibly attempt to kill her in a public place in front of so many witnesses. He has no idea the lengths this predator will go to kill its target, no matter who's around.

Later, after Sarah is taken to the police station, the lieutenant tells her, "There's a couch in this other room. Why don't you stretch out and try to get some sleep? . . . You'll be perfectly safe. We got thirty cops in this building."[2] They don't realize the Terminator can (and does) wipe them all out single-handedly. The problem isn't just that someone is out to kill her—it's that nobody understands the *power* of who is out to kill her.

In the passage of Scripture quoted at the start of this chapter, we read that God himself tells Cain that he doesn't know the power of the sin in his heart. The problem is not only that there is sin in the human heart—though, as the rest of the Bible makes clear, human sin is the primary reason for the world's condition—but also that we don't, and sometimes won't, recognize or acknowledge the *power* of sin. We underestimate it.

Therefore, there's nothing more important for us than understanding sin's true nature. God reveals to Cain—and to us—that nature in one vivid, pregnant utterance: "Sin is crouching at your door; it desires to have you, but you must master it."

We are told three things about sin in that one sentence. First, we are told that sin hides itself. It crouches. Second, we are told that sin is tremendously powerful. It wants nothing more than to have us. Third—and this is implicit in the sentence—we have hope against it. We must rule over it, master it. In one sentence, God tells us about the hiddenness of sin, the power of sin, and that there's a hope to defeat sin.

Sin Hides Itself by Nature

The Hebrew word for "crouching" solicits the image of wild beasts like leopards and tigers—usually large cats. If you have a cat, you know how they get around bugs. My family used to have a cat who wasn't much of a predator, but if she saw a bug flying around, she was suddenly back in the jungle. She would freeze. She would get out of sight, lie down low to make herself look much smaller than she actually was, and hide. She would crouch. Here, sin is depicted as something that hides just like this, although it's much more dangerous than a house cat.

What God tells Cain is that sin, by its nature, makes itself look smaller than it really is. In the midst of our ordinary lives and our ordinary feelings, a monster is hiding—and we often rationalize its effects on us. Let's look at the story of Cain and Abel to see how this works.

Early in the story, Cain experiences what seem to him like justifiable and, really, very ordinary feelings: "Cain was very angry, and his face was downcast" (Genesis 4:5). He was dejected and jealous of his brother—much like any of us would be if God seemed to prefer our sibling over us. This seems like a normal human response to being overshadowed by someone else.

But God tells Cain that he doesn't see what's at the heart of his own feelings. There is something crouching in the middle of that seemingly normal grudge. He has no clue how much power is hidden in that envy.

What's going on here? Cain and Abel both came to God with an offering. The word translated "offering" is important in understanding this story. There are a number of Hebrew words used to describe an offering, but the one that's used here, *minhah*, specifically means a gift or tribute offering.

A gift offering is not the same as a sin offering. Cain and Abel are not going to God for forgiveness here. Instead, they are taking something that belongs to them and giving it to God as a symbol that everything they own really belongs to him, including their whole selves.

A good example of a gift offering in contemporary Western culture is when a man wants to marry a woman so he gives her an engagement ring. During the wedding, the bride gives the groom a ring in return. As you probably know, these rings are very valuable. When I proposed to my wife, Kathy, both of us had to sell some of our books and pool our funds together to buy her engagement ring. We were starving students at the time, and getting the money together was difficult. But when a bride and groom exchange rings at a wedding, they're doing much more than just giving each other rings. They're saying, "This is a symbol of my giving myself to you." In fact, in the traditional Episcopal service (and this is a piece I always use when I do a wedding service), when the husband and wife put the ring on the other, they repeat after me, "I give you this ring as a symbol of my vow, and with all that I am and all that I have, I honor you." The ring is a token, a symbol, of giving all.

Let me ask you a question. What if a man went out, purchased a very expensive ring, brought it to his girlfriend, and said, "I give you this ring. Will you marry me?" She might say yes. But what if the night before, she found out he had been cheating on her? What is she going to say? "Why, thank you"?

No, she's going to say, "This isn't love; this is bribery. You're a liar. Maybe you *do* have feelings for me, but you won't give me your all. You want all of me with this offering, but you won't give me all of *you*. Forget it!"

If *we* dislike such a halfhearted gift, don't you think God does too? We may come to worship and give God all our prayers and money and offerings, but unless we back it up with our life, it's not love. It's not worship. It's bribery. It's a way of saying, "I would like God's favor, but I want to live my life my own way."

That's what Cain does here. How can we tell? Many people over the years have looked at the Mosaic law and its references to blood offerings and concluded that the problem is that Abel brings sheep while Cain brings grain. They say the issue in this passage is Cain's failure to bring a blood offering.

But that's not the issue here. To make a gift or tribute offering in those days, you brought something that symbolized whatever you did to make a living. Cain is a farmer; he brings produce. Abel is a shepherd; he brings sheep. There is nothing wrong with the *form* of the offering, with what each brought. The problem is something else. First John 3:12 gives us a clue. It specifies that "[Cain's] own actions were evil and his brother's were righteous." Why is that? The problem is what lies behind Cain's offering, with the state of his heart.

Cain's problem is that he is halfhearted, not wholehearted. That posture is tremendously common in the average churchgoer today. The average churchgoer is not a drug dealer. They're not running a prostitution ring. But they want to come to church and be moral and thereby pay God off while living life their own way, determining for themselves what is right and wrong. This is ordinary, lukewarm religion.

By contrast, Abel's religion is wholehearted. As a result, we are told that "the LORD had regard for Abel and his offering; but for Cain and his offering He had no regard" (Genesis 4:4–5 NASB). The word *regard* can be a little hard to understand in this context. Does it mean that after they make their offerings at the altar, a thunderous voice comes down from the heavens saying, "Abel? Great! Cain? Terrible!"? Probably not, since we are given direct quotations of what God said to Cain.

What is likely meant by "had no regard" for Cain is that God simply does not bless him and that Cain can tell this because his life isn't going well. In other words, God withdraws his favor from Cain, while Abel is blessed and loved. How does Cain respond? The King James Version says, "And Cain was very wroth, and his countenance fell" (v. 5). Or as the NIV translates it, "Cain was very angry, and his face was downcast."

The American theologian Cornelius Plantinga Jr. wrote a great book on sin called *Not the Way It's Supposed to Be: A Breviary of Sin*. In it he says that the core of the halfheartedness we are discussing—whether as seen in Cain or in the ordinary, lukewarm religion of our day—is viewing ourselves as our first cause and viewing God as an accessory to us. Sin is acting as if *we* are God. We try to use God as the means to meet our own ends: our own joy, our own happiness, our own agenda.[3]

When a true worshiper of God finds their life going poorly, they grow confused and ask, "Lord, why?" But when life doesn't go well for a briber of God, they get exceedingly wroth. They say, "This isn't right—and I have a right for things to go my way." At the heart of this attitude is a demandingness—a sense of entitlement, as if God owes us whatever we want. As if life owes us whatever we want. That little seed of entitlement, if left unchecked, will grow. You'll start trampling on people to get what's best for you. You'll get angry and do whatever it takes to get what you seek. The monster hiding in this halfheartedness will show itself whenever life doesn't go your way.

This halfheartedness, this unwillingness to say, "You're God and I'm not," is very common. It's even ordinary for most of us. But in it are the seeds of something terrible. God goes to Cain and says, in effect, "In this envy is hidden murder. Don't you see what's crouching at your door? It looks ordinary, but it's not. It's a monster."

Sin Hides Itself Intellectually

When I ask the average person how humanity could be capable of the Holocaust or how teenagers could commit contract killings or why Bosnian concentration camps existed, most people give the same answer. They say that those instances are exceptions and that ordinary people aren't capable of such evils and that most of us are inherently good.

In the 1960s, a former Nazi and organizer of the Holocaust named Adolf Eichmann was arrested after he was found hiding in Argentina. What many found unnerving about Eichmann—and indeed many other Nazis tried for war crimes—was how ordinary he appeared. When Hannah Arendt, a German American political theorist, reported on Eichmann's trial for the atrocities he committed, she coined the now-famous phrase "the banality of evil" to convey his seeming ordinariness, despite what he had done.

We want to believe ordinary people can't do monstrous things—that only the truly evil ones do things like that.

But when we see the monsters, we see that they're like us. They're ordinary. If *they* are capable, *we* are capable. Historically, we want to believe that ordinary people are all right, but the Bible tells us that at the heart of the ordinary is a monster.

In *The Roosevelt I Knew*, the memoirs of Frances Perkins, the secretary of labor for President Franklin D. Roosevelt, Perkins tells a fascinating story that illustrates the difficulty we often have believing that a regular, ordinary person could be capable of such evil. Roosevelt received many reports about incredible atrocities happening in Europe during the early years of World War II, but he didn't listen to them. He didn't really believe what he was hearing and chose not to deal with it.

When it dawned on Roosevelt that the reports were not exaggerated, he was at a loss as to how normal human beings could act so evilly. In early 1944 he went to church at Hyde Park, where an Episcopalian minister asked him if he had read Danish theologian Søren Kierkegaard's writings on original sin. Roosevelt began to read them. Not long after that, he called Perkins into his office and asked her, "Have you ever read Kierkegaard? Well, you ought to read him. It will teach you about the Nazis. Kierkegaard explains the Nazis to me as nothing else ever has. I have never been able to make out why people who are obviously human beings could behave like that. . . . Kierkegaard gives you an understanding of what is in man that makes it possible for these Germans to be so evil."[4] In other words, a normal, liberal, secular humanist like Roosevelt could not believe human beings were capable of doing what he was hearing. For the situation to be comprehensible, he had to read—and be amazed by—Kierkegaard's explanation of what the Bible teaches us about original sin. Without that biblical teaching, Roosevelt was out of touch with reality and therefore unprepared to handle life.

Sin Hides Itself Personally

Our own worst sins look much smaller to us than they do to anyone else. If we have good people in our lives who really know us, like a great spouse or great friends who tell us the truth, they can see our shortcomings much more clearly than we ever could. If you ask them to point out your flaws, you will be amazed at how evident your shortcomings are to them when they're barely visible to you. We never see what is obvious to others.

This is why it's so important to live life alongside people who can help you see what you can't. Today, many people—especially those in cities, but it is true everywhere—live alone or away from family, close friends, or anyone who sees them day in and day out. If this is the case with you, find a small group at a church that will offer you the chance to grow close to others who can be of help. All of us need people who can see in us what we cannot see in ourselves.

This is crucial because if we leave our sins unaddressed, they will grow larger than we could ever imagine. Every grudge wants to be murder. Every lust wants to be adultery. Every envy wants to be robbery. Every self-pity is an idolatry of something you're sure will save you—something more important than God.

Our sin tells us it won't hurt us and that we deserve what it offers, and so we give it quarter. We tolerate it. This is exactly what God is trying to warn us about in this passage. He's calling us to master our sin, to "rule over it" (Genesis 4:7 NKJV). The old Puritans had an expression: "Have quit with sin." That meant to have nothing to do with it. Don't give it any spot in your life. Don't just say to yourself, "It'll be okay. I see it over there in the corner. It's really rather small. In fact, I think it's asleep." Don't do that.

Throughout history, the hiddenness of sin has fooled every society and every culture. Don't let it fool you too. Tolerate it not a bit.

Sin's Desire Is to Have Us

In Genesis 4:7, God says to Cain, "If you do not do what is right, sin is crouching at your door." This speaks to a powerful reality: When we don't do what is right, we create something that haunts us and chews on us.

Let me put it in a pithy little way: After you've done a sin, the sin does you. Sin is not done with you after you're done with it. When you sin, it doesn't just pass away; it takes on a life of its own and wants to devour you. Sin has a power and vitality to it. And its job is to have you.

Throughout the rest of the book, we'll examine how exactly sin can have us, but for now let me give you an example of this two-sided power of sin. After you tell a lie, you're not suddenly done with lying. You will find you have to lie again to maintain the first lie you told. You don't have to be a Christian and believe the Bible to know this dynamic; plenty of wise thinkers and religions have all acknowledged it. Sin has an addictive power. It's like the old advertising claim of Lay's potato chips: You can't stop at just one. When you lie, you find you *have* to do it again. And when you lie again, you'll also find that it's easier than it was the first time. It's amazing how fast the unthinkable becomes thinkable after we find ourselves doing it.

The same is true of hate. If you hate, the hate grows. You want more of it. This is why C. S. Lewis argued that, at first, the Nazis killed the Jews because they hated them, but eventually, they hated them because they were killing them.[5] Do you see what he means? When we misuse somebody because we're mad at them, we find ourselves compelled to stay mad at them to justify what we've done. It becomes a cyclical habit that we can't simply slip out of. Before we know it, the behavior has overtaken us. Haters are eaten up by hatred. Liars are eaten up by lies.

John Steinbeck wrote a fascinating novel called *East of Eden*. It's about a man named Adam whose life has been destroyed by a competitive rivalry with his brother Charles.

Adam then marries and moves to California to set up a new home where he'll finally have a happy life. He has two sons named Caleb and Aron. Sounds a lot like Cain and Abel, doesn't it? That is intentional.

As his life unfolds, Adam finds to his horror that the problem in his life wasn't Charles—it was himself. The pride and competitiveness in his own heart pass down into the hearts of his children. Instead of loving and sharing with each other, they're just as hostile as Adam and Charles were. The sin keeps on going, and it becomes more pronounced as it goes.

But there is more to this dynamic than just the addictive power of sin. If you lie, not only will it become easier, even compulsory, to lie more; you will also find yourself being lied *to*. When you lie, not only does something happen *inside* you, but something happens *outside* you.

This is what Cornelius Plantinga calls the "law of returns":

No matter what we sow, the law of returns applies.

Good or evil, love or hate, justice or tyranny, grapes or thorns, a gracious compliment or a peevish complaint—whatever we invest, we tend to get it back with interest. Lovers are loved; haters, hated. Forgivers usually get forgiven; those who live by the sword die by the sword. "God is not mocked, for you reap whatever you sow" [Galatians 6:7].[6]

This is the way God made the universe. When we go against God's law, we go against ourselves. Sin is not just wrong; it's stupid. It goes against not just the grain of our souls but also the grain of the entire universe.

Liars end up being lied to. Gossips are always gossiped about. Haters will always be hated back. Betrayers will be betrayed. Cowards will be deserted. Why? It may not happen immediately, every day, or at every moment, but eventually we always reap what we sow. Our sins are not done with us when we're done with them. They will stop at nothing to overtake us.

There's Hope for Sin

Some of you may be reading this and thinking, "Where's the hope? This is such a bleak introduction. Why am I reading this?" I have good news. The Terminator may be after us, but there is something much greater that can save us from it. There is a Savior who can help us. At one point in the film, when Sarah is on the verge of being terminated, someone approaches her and says, "Come with me if you want to live." The Bible tells us the same thing. Sin is after us, and we'll never be able to save ourselves from it on our own. So what do we do? Although God says we must master it, he doesn't exactly show us how. Let me explain what's going on here.

First, God comes to Cain. Don't overlook this. There is hope in the fact that God appeals to Cain. I love this conversation. He says, "Why are you angry? Why is your face downcast?" (Genesis 4:6). In essence he's asking Cain, "Don't you see what's going on?" What can we learn about God from these questions? For one, we can tell his approach is much different from those of the ministers and Christians whose attitudes toward sinners are terribly condemning. When we read about God conversing with sinners, what does he say? God asks Adam and Eve, "Where are you?" asking them, in essence, to tell him what has gone wrong. He asks Jonah, "Have you any right to be angry?" And here he invites Cain into a conversation, as if to say, "Now Cain, let's think about this." These responses from God are amazing. There is a challenge and an honesty about the seriousness of sin—but there is also hope.

It's as though God is saying, "Cain, can't you see that Abel is not your real enemy? Sin is your real enemy. Your real problem is not what I've done to you or what your brother has done to you. You're not miserable because of what has happened to you. You're miserable because of what's *in* you. Don't you see, Cain? You're not a victim. But there's hope. There's something you can do about it."

God offers this same question and counsel to all of us. We may have been mistreated, but it is our self-pity, our anger, our bitterness, our refusal to forgive, our pride, our hurt feelings, or our insistence that certain things will save us that makes us truly miserable.

God comes to us and challenges us to repent because it's the only answer to our problem that carries real hope. If sin is our problem, we can work with God to master it. If our problem is solely what is outside of us—as Cain thought, believing his problem was Abel—then our options are limited. Even the most extreme responses will ultimately fail to solve the problem, as Cain's murder of Abel reveals. But if the problem is the sin *in us*, then we stand a chance to do something that will help solve it. Do you hear God coming to you and giving you this hopeful challenge?

Even after Cain murders Abel, God comes to him again and asks, "Where is your brother?" (Genesis 4:9). God isn't looking for information. He already knows what happened. He's looking for repentance. He's giving Cain one last chance to repent. There is hope if he can see the sin, stop blaming Abel and God and everything else for his own sorrow, and say, "I'm miserable because of my sin."

But Cain says the most horrible thing he could say. He coldheartedly says, in contemporary terms, "Am I Abel's babysitter?" That response makes clear that sin has already devoured him.

What does God say? "Your brother's blood cries out to me from the ground" (v. 10). Human blood is not so easily washed away as ink or water. When a human being is killed, a wealth of evidence is left behind. This is an illustration of an underlying reality. Because human beings are valuable, because creation is good, God cannot pass over sin. When we, in our sin, destroy relationships, reputations, or lives themselves, the ruins of God's creation cry out to him.

God can't let such destruction go unaccounted for.

Why? Because he stands for peace. He stands for harmony. He stands for love. He is for the goodness of his creation. For him not to listen to the cry of the blood on the ground would be for him to treat human beings as if they were trash. Because Cain won't repent, God shows him Abel's blood.

It's tempting to wonder, "What if Cain *had* repented?" But let's turn the question back to ourselves. What if *we* repent? What if today we finally say, "You know what? My problems *are* because of my sin. The main problem in my life *is* my sin, not what has been done to me." What will happen? God will take you to a pool of blood too—a pool of blood that's crying out—but it won't be Abel's. And this is where hope is found.

Abel was only the first in a long line of wholehearted people who were killed or persecuted because they challenged, convicted, or showed up their halfhearted brothers. When somebody comes along who's wholehearted and pure, we hate them because they make the rest of us look bad. They're the smartest student who performs well on the test and kills the grading curve for the rest of us. Abel was the first to do this. Joseph was another hated by his brothers and persecuted. David was despised by Saul and persecuted. Stephen was a great religious leader killed by the other religious leaders.

But the ultimate Abel was Jesus. He's not just *like* Abel; he's the ultimate Abel. He wasn't just good. He was perfect. He didn't just die *by our hands*—he died, voluntarily, *for our sin*. Hebrews 12:23–24 says, "You have come to . . . Jesus the mediator of a new covenant, and to the sprinkled blood that speaks a better word than the blood of Abel." All human blood cries out for justice, and so does Jesus's. But Jesus's blood cries out in a different way than any other. Because he was perfect and died for our sins as our substitute, Jesus's blood cries to God "a better word" than anyone else's.

If we repent, God takes us to Jesus's blood—and it petitions God to bless us with his grace, his mercy, and his salvation. It cries out, "Father, sin must be paid. I have paid for the sins of those who believe in me. It would be unjust for you to punish them, lest you receive two payments." If we don't repent, the blood of everyone else we've hurt—the ruins of all we've destroyed—cries out against us, saying, "In the name of justice, reject them!" Jesus's is the only blood that cries out, "In the name of justice, save them. Embrace them. Love them. I have paid for them." Without Jesus, God's justice is against us. With Jesus, God's justice can be *for* us.

Maybe you've never acknowledged your sin. Maybe you've never repented. Maybe you're like Cain—you're religious to a degree, but you've never wanted to go all the way when it comes to submitting yourself to God. If you've ever heard yourself say, "I'm religious, but I'm not fanatical about it," look out! Watch for what's in your heart of hearts: a desire to *be* God rather than to be *under* God.

If any of those descriptions apply to you, hear God's words and don't underestimate the predator that wants to claim you. If you repent, God will take you to Jesus's blood, which is crying out on your behalf. If you don't, you choose for yourself a much more tragic future in this life: a restless wandering in which you will always wonder why you are never satisfied—just like Cain.

Recall how at the end of the passage Cain says that someone will surely kill him for what he's done. The truth is, he deserves to be killed. He murdered someone, after all. But what does God do? He shows Cain compassion even then: "Then the LORD put a mark on Cain so that no one who found him would kill him" (Genesis 4:15).

God will, to the end of your life, continue to care about you and preserve you and keep you from getting what your sins deserve. He cares that much about you. Go to him. Only then, through the saving work of Jesus Christ, can you master that which seeks to destroy you.

A PRAYER FOR REPENTANCE

I ask now, Father, that you would help me see what I have to do to bring myself before you and say, "I repent. It is my fault." Lord, if you came to Cain when he was in sin and treated him so gently, how much more gently will you treat me if I come to you in repentance? If you are so kind to Cain even as he murders, how kind will you be if I confess my sins?

Lord, I ask that the blood of Christ would speak graciously to you on my behalf and that it would free me as I look and see what he has done for me. He was devoured by my sin; therefore, I don't have to be. I pray, Lord, that the love and mercy and grace of this sacrifice will affect me so I find that, in the knowledge of your love for me, I really can master the sin that crouches down. Help me to do so. I pray in Jesus's name. Amen.

SIN AS SELF-DECEPTION

1 Samuel 15:12–23

¹² Early in the morning Samuel got up and went to meet Saul, but he was told, "Saul has gone to Carmel. There he has set up a monument in his own honor and has turned and gone on down to Gilgal."

¹³ When Samuel reached him, Saul said, "The LORD bless you! I have carried out the LORD's instructions."

¹⁴ But Samuel said, "What then is this bleating of sheep in my ears? What is this lowing of cattle that I hear?"

¹⁵ Saul answered, "The soldiers brought them from the Amalekites; they spared the best of the sheep and cattle to sacrifice to the LORD your God, but we totally destroyed the rest."

¹⁶ "Stop!" Samuel said to Saul. "Let me tell you what the LORD said to me last night."

"Tell me," Saul replied.

¹⁷ Samuel said, "Although you were once small in your own eyes, did you not become the head of the tribes of Israel? The LORD anointed you king over Israel. ¹⁸ And he sent you on a mission, saying, 'Go and completely destroy those wicked people, the Amalekites; make war on them until you have wiped them out.' ¹⁹ Why did you not obey the LORD? Why did you pounce on the plunder and do evil in the eyes of the LORD?"

²⁰ "But I did obey the LORD," Saul said. "I went on the mission the LORD assigned me. I completely destroyed the Amalekites and brought back Agag their king. ²¹ The soldiers took sheep and cattle from the plunder, the best of what was devoted to God, in order to sacrifice them to the LORD your God at Gilgal."

²² But Samuel replied:

"Does the LORD delight in burnt offerings and
        sacrifices
    as much as in obeying the voice of the LORD?

To obey is better than sacrifice,

and to heed is better than the fat of rams.

²³ For rebellion is like the sin of divination,

and arrogance like the evil of idolatry.

Because you have rejected the word of the LORD,

he has rejected you as king."

We explored in the previous chapter how sin's power as a predator is heightened by our underestimation of it. In this chapter we will look at another magnifier of sin's power: our capacity for self-deception. This aspect of sin is extremely important to understand: the almost infinite ability of the human heart to deceive itself, especially when the truth is too uncomfortable to confront.

One of the things that surprised me as I was researching this topic is that, since the 1960s, journals of professional philosophy have spent a tremendous amount of time on the philosophical issue of self-deception. It hasn't been just Christians and religious people talking about it. There has been a great deal of high-level, scholarly discussion on this matter.

At first I thought, "Why in the world would self-deception be such an important concept for scholars?" Then I read more and found out why. Consider someone who has a problem with alcoholism. What is it that truly hurts them more: their addiction to alcohol or their denial of being addicted to alcohol? It is arguably the latter, if only because denial enables all kinds of other problems. Self-deception may not be the worst thing we do, but it's what makes us capable of terrible things.

There's no better example of the tragedy of self-deception in the Bible than this story of Saul, the first king of Israel. This text tells us about the reality of self-deception, shows the structure of it, and even gives us a prescription to be healed of it.

The Reality of Self-Deception

To understand the reality of self-deception presented in this passage, we need to understand Saul's history with the prophet Samuel. Verses 11 and 12 say that Samuel gets up very early because he hasn't slept all night. Why hasn't he?

Samuel had anointed Saul as the first king of Israel. He had mentored him and loved him. It was hard *not* to love Saul. If you read the rest of the Bible's descriptions of him, you'll know he was an exuberant, emotionally expressive man. Many people loved him because of that enthusiasm. But a sinful pattern had reared up in his life, and as this pattern continued, the incident in this passage brought it to a head.

In the early part of 1 Samuel 15, God reveals himself to Saul by a prophecy and tells him to "attack the Amalekites and totally destroy everything that belongs to them" (v. 3). The Amalekites were a nation of incredibly violent people who had committed all sorts of atrocities to profit and enrich themselves. You may remember that when the Israelites first escaped from Egypt, the Amalekites attacked them. But the Amalekites didn't target the front of the group, where the soldiers were. They attacked the stragglers at the rear: the ill, the elderly, the pregnant, and the new mothers. So in his instructions to Saul, God was sending the Amalekites a reckoning for what they had done, something God had promised Moses he would do (Deuteronomy 25:17–19). God sent Saul to engage the Amalekites in battle and specifically instructed him to take no prisoners and take none of their wealth. If he found their treasure, he was to throw it out. If he found their livestock, he was to slaughter it. God would not let Saul profit one bit from this battle.

Why did God make this stipulation? Because God is sending Saul to perform an act of justice, not an act of imperialism. When a group of people like the Amalekites is marauding and pillaging and murdering, justice demands that they be stopped. God tells Saul to ensure that what he does is an act of justice, not a recapitulation of the very thing the

Amalekites had done. God wants Israel's actions to be just, unlike the countless nations that have gone off to war in the name of truth and justice but desired nothing more than to profit from the spoils of war.

So Saul went to war and defeated them. God helped him in the battle. But afterward, Saul captured the Amalekite king, Agag, saving his life, and brought home the majority of the Amalekite livestock—the best of their wealth.

Saul must have thought, "I've done 99 percent of what God asked me to do. I killed all of them but Agag. I slaughtered everything but the best of the sheep. That should be plenty." In actuality, however, Saul had not done 99 percent of what God asked. He did 0 percent. He became like his own enemy. He did the very thing that the Amalekites were to be punished for.

In William Shakespeare's *Henry V*, before the battle of the English and the French at Agincourt, there's a long discussion about how regular soldiers were often slaughtered, while nobles, kings, and officers were usually captured. Those in the latter groups are worth money, of course, and so they were often ransomed.[1] See the inequity of it? Wars are always fought under the pretense of a just cause, but at the end of the day, many, perhaps most, are simply grabs for power and wealth.

Saul did the very thing God hates—and he'd been doing it all along. It was a pattern of behavior for Saul as we can see from God's message to Samuel. God spoke to Samuel at night and told him he'd had enough. Saul had been becoming the very kind of king that is a stench in God's nostrils, and finally he'd arrived. God told Samuel, "I am grieved that I have made Saul king, because he has turned away from me and has not carried out my instructions" (1 Samuel 15:11). And he decided to no longer honor Saul as king of his people.

We're also told in verse 11 that Samuel was up all night crying and praying out of tremendous grief. He loved Saul. When he went to see him in the morning, Saul greeted him with an unusually enthusiastic and excited response: "The LORD bless you! I have carried out the LORD's instructions." This greeting would raise anyone's suspicions. To paraphrase Lady Gertrude in *Hamlet*, "King Saul doth protest too much."

And then Saul went further. He said to Samuel, in essence, "What a fine day! The Lord is with us. He has blessed us with this victory—the first time we've been victorious over another country. Oh, what a great day this is going to be. I'm preparing the greatest worship celebration you've ever seen. We have the sacrifices all prepared, and I want *you* to preach the sermon."

This is stunning, isn't it? Saul's posture perfectly illustrates the power of self-deception. Here's the reality: Saul was oblivious, and yet he wasn't. Self-deception is the ability to know the truth and yet *not* know it because you don't want to. Self-deception is the tendency to rationalize and justify things we know are wrong. When we deceive ourselves, we always see the truth, but it's too painful to accept. It's too hot to hold. There's evidence that we know whatever we are denying is true, but we smother that knowledge using various techniques, which we'll examine shortly. Saul knew he hadn't done what he was supposed to—and yet he worked hard to convince himself he had.

The Structure of Self-Deception

We deceive ourselves in many different ways and in many different circumstances, ranging from the trivial and comic to the dire and serious. As an example of the former, I will confess I always have trouble believing there's anything wrong with my car. Kathy and I will be driving along, and Kathy will say, "Do you hear that noise? Something is wrong with the car. We'd better take it to a mechanic." Now, we have only one car, so handing it over to a mechanic is awfully inconvenient: the money, the time, the inability to drive anywhere. So how do I respond?

I say, "Honey, you're so pessimistic. Cars always do this. I know more about cars. You've never worked on cars," and then I turn the radio up. And right there is the evidence that I know something's wrong with the car. I turn that radio up because I don't *want* to know there's something wrong. And then I go further and say to Kathy, "You're a glass-half-empty person. I'm a glass-half-full person." And I keep driving.

This is a comic illustration of our capacity for self-deception, but others are more serious. Imagine a father who has a son. Over the last two years, other kids have accused his little Johnny of stealing money four different times in four different places. Each time, the father storms onto the scene and tells the parents of the accusers that the children are simply jealous of Johnny, who is the best athlete in town. The truth is that his son is a thief, but it's too painful for him to accept. There's evidence that he knows the truth: He locks up his own wallet. But he smothers the truth.

Or imagine a woman who is a talented musician raised in a fairly religious home, then moves to New York to break into the rock music scene. Deep down she knows that there *is* a God, that there *is* a right and wrong, and that there *are* moral absolutes. There's plenty of evidence that this is the case. For instance, she says that racism is objectively wrong, revealing that she believes in moral absolutes that apply to everyone—absolutes that must have been put in place by a Creator. But it's painful for her to acknowledge that. She desperately wants to be accepted, to be seen as cool, to get the gig she wants, to hang out with the right people. And she certainly wants to keep her boyfriend, who wants to sleep with her.

So she hides the truth that she really believes. Whenever anyone brings up belief in God, she tells the person (and herself), "Eh, most of the Christians I know are hypocrites."

Here's a final example. At the end of World War II as the Allies were moving through Germany, General Eisenhower grew tired of the fact that, whenever he visited towns near camps where incredible atrocities had occurred, the towns-people and local officials would claim to have known nothing about it.[2] In one particular town, Eisenhower reached a boiling point. He issued a command: Every man, woman, and child in that town would march into the camp at gunpoint and bury the bodies themselves. The townspeople did so and, when they were finished, went back to their homes. That night the mayor and his wife hanged themselves. Why? Because they had known the truth. And they could no longer hide from themselves what they had known all along but didn't want to face.

We have an infinite capacity to lie to ourselves. If we don't like the truth, we develop ways *not* to know it. We use at least three techniques to smother what we know. In this passage from 1 Samuel, we see that Saul uses all three.

A First Technique: Blaming Others

After Samuel asks, "What then is this bleating of sheep in my ears?" (1 Samuel 15:14), Saul answers by saying, "The soldiers brought them from the Amalekites" (v. 15). That's quite a response. One is tempted to ask, "Who was in charge here, Saul?" But it's clear what he is doing: He's blaming someone else for his own faults. This is the first technique of self-deception.

This is the technique I use in the car with Kathy, telling her she's a pessimist. That may be a rather small kind of blaming, but it's blaming all the same. And when you get comfortable blaming others, the excuses grow larger and larger. The father of the thief says the other kids are just jealous. The rock singer says that all those Christians are hypocrites. In all these cases, somebody else has done something wrong and my own sin gets overlooked.

Does that mean there *aren't* Christians who are hypocrites? Of course not. Some doctors are quacks, but that doesn't mean the very science of medicine is wrong. And we wouldn't argue that. But that's the point: We selectively blame others to blind ourselves to reality.

We do this in many different ways. For example, I have known people who do not want to get married because they are scared to death of committing themselves to an imperfect person. But they don't want to think of themselves as cowardly, so every time a relationship gets serious, they find something wrong with the other person and call it quits. They can look back on the ten times they've been engaged and see they broke off every single engagement. Yet they find it all too easy to think, "Wow, ten times I have dated a real loser." Blaming others, as Saul did, is a common technique for self-deception.

A Second Technique: Focusing Only on Our Goodness

The second method for deceiving ourselves is to make the same argument to ourselves that Saul did to Samuel when he said the livestock were spared "to sacrifice to the LORD"

(1 Samuel 15:15). Saul's response to Samuel is, essentially, "I did this wrong, sure, but look at all the right I'm doing." This technique is frighteningly common.

To avoid confronting the truth that he didn't follow God's instructions, Saul brings up the idea that he's going to do something good to make up for it. We've all heard the phrase "Two wrongs don't make a right." The technique used here might be summarized as "Several rights make up for the wrong I continue to do." It's as if he says to Samuel, "Yes, yes, I did bring the sheep, but I'm going to donate them." This attitude is commonplace in history. Do you have any idea how many of the great church buildings have been funded by individuals who made their money by trampling on people and then said to themselves, "Maybe I wasn't obedient in this or that area, but the important thing is that I'm going to do good by making a sacrifice. I'm going to fund a building for the Lord."

Many of us lie to ourselves this way. We find something that shows we're a good person and focus on it. Maybe we're good to our mother. Maybe we give to charity. Better to think about that, we say, instead of that sin we have over in the corner. Some of you may be reading this and telling yourselves, "I know I'm doing some things wrong, but I'm a Bible study leader, and I'm a volunteer, and I do other things in the church. I do so many good things!" It doesn't matter what you do, who you are, or what position you hold—these don't excuse or make up for your sin. Saul was the king of

Israel, but his position didn't help him. In fact, it made it worse.

Elisabeth Elliot, a twentieth-century missionary and author, tells a story about this type of behavior. When she was a young girl, her mother told her little brother Tommy (who grew up to become the highly regarded theologian Thomas Howard) that he was allowed to play with all the paper bags that were underneath the counter in the kitchen. He could spread them all out and do whatever he wanted with them, but he had to put them back. He couldn't leave the kitchen without cleaning them up.

One day Tommy spread them all out and didn't put them away. He left the kitchen to listen to his father play the piano. When his mother came into the kitchen and saw the mess, she told him to come pick up the bags.

Tommy replied in his small voice, "But I wanna sing 'Jesus Loves Me.'"

His father said, "It's not good singing God's praises if you're being disobedient. To obey is better than sacrifice."[3] Does the Lord delight in burnt offerings and donations and helping the poor when we are refusing to actually obey what he tells us to do? We tell ourselves that our good deeds compensate for our disobedience, and so we try to deceive ourselves.

A Third Technique: Minimizing Our Sin

The third method of self-deception is to look at what we've done wrong and minimize it. In our heads, we twist what we've done to make it seem insignificant. In verse 20, Saul says, "But I did obey the LORD. . . . I went on the mission the LORD assigned me. I completely destroyed the Amalekites and brought back Agag their king." Notice how he twists this: I *did* completely wipe them out, and I *also* did this other thing. The argument is that what he did wrong should not diminish the fact that he also did what God wanted.

Samuel points out that, no, Saul *didn't* do completely what he was told: He kept the king alive and failed to destroy the plunder. In other words, he failed to deliver justice to the Amalekites completely.

We can easily imagine Saul's internal monologue, which will be familiar to many of us. "Well, I *virtually* did it completely. I did what I was told completely, and I added to it. The only thing I did wrong was so little that it should not mean I can't use the word *completely*. I just added to it."

We minimize our sin in other ways too. Often we do so by comparing it to other people's actions that seem much worse. Notice how midway through Saul's defense of his actions, he makes it sound like what the soldiers did was worse. "I completely destroyed the Amalekites and brought back Agag their king. The soldiers took sheep and cattle from the plunder" (vv. 20–21). Saul may have taken one king, sure, but the soldiers took a whole lot of sheep and cattle.

We all do this. We say to ourselves and often to others, "What I did may have been wrong, but it's not that big of a deal. Just look at what those people are doing." An independent business owner may cheat on his taxes and think, "Well, at least I'm not like one of those Fortune 500 CEOs with a hundred charges of fraud. I'm not making nearly as much as them." What does the CEO who embezzles think? "It's all just dollars and cents. It's not like I'm killing people like some mafia hit man." What does the hit man think? "Come on, it's not like I'm Hitler. I only kill people who deserve it." And Hitler undoubtedly thought something just the same. And on and on it goes.

The Reason for Self-Deception

Three of the most prevalent ways we smother truth are blaming others, focusing only on our goodness, and minimizing our sin. We can't be healed of self-deception until we recognize these techniques for what they are. But there is something else we need to uncover. Samuel's response to Saul reveals a dynamic that operates underneath these techniques, one that is crucial for us to see if we want to avoid them.

As noted earlier, we don't deceive ourselves about *all* truths—only painful ones. But here's the question. *Why* are some truths psychologically painful? Why can't the father admit his son is a thief? Why can't the alcoholic admit he drinks too much? Why can't the business owner admit he's a cheat? Samuel reveals the reason in verse 17: "Although you were once small in your own eyes, did you not become the head of the tribes of Israel? The LORD anointed you king over Israel." Do you see it? Saul was small, but the Lord made him great. So why, Samuel is asking Saul, are you trying to make yourself great? Recall that in verse 12, Samuel, on his way to find Saul, is told that the king has put up a monument in his own honor. This, along with Saul's capture of Agag, shows where Saul's true motivations lie.

In this time period, if someone defeated a king, they never killed him. They kept the king alive because that made them a king of kings. It made them an emperor. Saul desperately wanted to be included in the culture of emperors. He didn't want to be king of just Israel. He wanted to be a king that the other kings saw and respected and feared. So now, he thinks, when he has finally defeated a nation in battle, how could he possibly let go of this opportunity to grow bigger, wealthier, and more famous? Things are finally falling his way.

Saul says he did all of this for the Lord, but what Samuel tells him forces him to unmask himself. Saul still thinks he's small, even though God in his grace has already made him great and will continue to make him great. But Saul rejects the grace of God and tries to do it himself. He turns to the world to get something only God can give. As a result, there are some things he cannot allow himself to admit.

This is our whole problem. We're sinners. We know deep down that we're small, and this is the fundamental reason we deceive ourselves. We find ways to try to hide from ourselves the truth that we are sinners, that we're small, that we're inadequate, and that we're flawed. If any truth comes along to reveal our sin, we can't stomach it. We feel that no alternative exists other than to make ourselves big.

The father can't stand to know Johnny is a thief because the father's image of himself as a good father is the only thing he has to save himself. It's the only way he can say, "I'm not small. I'm not some nothing in this huge universe. I'm a good father." He can't live without that idea, so he must repress anything that goes against it. So too with all of us.

Samuel comes to Saul and asks, *Do you realize your rebellion is idolatry?* Saul was likely telling himself all sorts of rationalizations. *I'm doing as the Lord asks. It's not like I'm an idol worshiper. I'm not like those people practicing witchcraft.* But what does Samuel say in verse 23? "For rebellion is like the sin of divination, and arrogance like the evil of idolatry."

Saul's idol is worldly esteem and power. The father's idol is the image of himself as a perfect father. The rock singer's idol is the acceptance of her peers.

We all go to our idols and say, *Make me big,* because deep inside we know we are small. But don't we see what Samuel tells us? Our own efforts will never make us truly great—nor will anything else we can get from the world. It is only by the grace of God that we are made more than something small. And this leads to our final question, which, in a sense, we've already answered: How do we heal?

The Healing from Self-Deception

The first thing we must do to heal ourselves from self-deception is what Samuel did the moment he started talking to Saul: pointing out the bleating. In other words, Samuel identifies the evidence of self-deception.

We must look for the evidence in our own lives. But as I mentioned earlier, I don't believe most self-deceived people can see this evidence on their own. That is why it's so important for us to involve trusted figures in our lives who can give us a better perspective of ourselves. Many people are resistant to this. Some people believe they must face their struggles alone—individuals who do, in fact, have problems but feel they can't ever tell anybody about them. They believe they can handle their problems on their own or think that the idea of being vulnerable and open to constructive feedback is a burden too heavy to bear. They don't want to join a small group at their church, see a counselor, or even talk to a friend.

This is the type of person who underestimates the power of self-deception. Who better to see self-deception than someone who's not the self? If you find yourself not wanting to share with anyone or become accountable, watch out. These are telltale signs of self-deception.

Again, find the evidence. If you notice you always make exceptions for yourself—if you're always telling yourself, "Well, I know I should forgive, but I was provoked," or "I know I should obey the Bible, but, you know, a lot of people question whether that one section really means what it says"—or employ any of the techniques listed previously, see this behavior for what it is and make a note of it.

Second, remember this: If you're prone to self-deception, that means you don't want to see uncomfortable truths. A self-deceiver is somebody who refuses to think through the implications of what they inwardly know to be true. In other words, you know a reality deep within yourself, but you don't want to think about what it means. You're afraid of the implications and stifle them before you can even discern what they are.

At the heart of self-deception is a refusal to handle the most earth-shattering truth of all. If there is a God, he owns you utterly and you must obey him completely. If there is no God, your life is meaningless and nothing is truly right or wrong and no one knows which end is up.

We don't want the latter to be true, of course. But many of us don't want the former to be true either, because if it is, it means total submission. It means we can't just say, "I'm going to live my life how I want, but I'll be sure to put some money in the offering plate." The options are complete obedience to the One who created us or meaninglessness. There is nothing in between. If you want to be healed of self-deception, you *must* be willing to think about the implications of this truth, no matter how daunting it seems. We must force that on ourselves. We must explore the idea of what it means to give ourselves to God—and the idea that God wants us.

God didn't want Saul's cattle. He didn't want his sheep. He wanted *him*, just as he wants us. But all too often, we withhold ourselves. When we reserve the right to decide when to obey, we're really telling God, "Sorry, but you can't have me." To give ourselves is to say unconditionally, "I will obey." There is no space to say, "I only disobeyed this part of what I was told to do," or "It wasn't a big deal," or "Other people do much worse." It doesn't matter if we disobey a million times out of a million or once out of a million. The point is the same. We didn't give ourselves to God completely. And he indeed wants us—completely.

Last of all, we must come to grips with grace. Over the years, I've tried to help many people with self-deception, and I've come to this conclusion: We all know in our hearts that we're sinners. We don't want to see it. But if we do not understand the grace of God, we *can't* escape self-deception. It is inevitable.

The grace of God says that God will make us big. Saul might have heard that and wondered how it was possible. Because he didn't believe it, he disobeyed. But we know something he didn't know. We see it spelled out in Hebrews 10:5–7:

Therefore, when Christ came into the world, he said:

"Sacrifice and offering you did not desire,
 but a body you prepared for me;

44

> with burnt offerings and sin offerings
>> you were not pleased.
> Then I said, 'Here I am—it is written about me
>> in the scroll—
> I have come to do your will, O God.'"

The writer of Hebrews goes on to say, "By that will, we have been made holy through the sacrifice of the body of Jesus Christ once for all" (v. 10). We have to understand this or we'll never stop trying to fool ourselves. Jesus was great and became small so we who are small might be made great. But why would God take weak, cowardly sinners like us and anoint us all kings and priests, as Revelation 5:10 says?

This may have been difficult for Saul to grasp, but it shouldn't be so for us. We have the knowledge that when Jesus Christ died, he did so with perfect obedience as the perfect sacrifice. God was delighted with the life Jesus lived. And when we believe in Christ and his atonement, we are given access to that same delight. God delights in us.

If we know that Jesus succeeded on our behalf where we failed, if we grasp the grace that God has for us and that he wants nothing more than to have us and delight in us, we can handle the truth about ourselves. We can handle that our son is a thief. We can handle that some of the members of the rock cognoscenti will reject us. We can handle that sometimes we're cowardly or blame others or diminish our own sins. We can handle it all . . . finally. The grace of God liberates us. We will know the truth, and the truth will set us free from trying to make ourselves great through our own actions. We are already kings and priests. Does God delight in burnt offerings and sacrifices as he does in us obeying his voice? Jesus obeyed perfectly so God can be delighted in you.

A PRAYER AGAINST SELF-DECEPTION

Father, give me the power to take off all my masks, to break through my self-defenses, and to see the ways in which I deceive myself. Oh Lord, I realize that in the end it's not simply a matter of noticing the techniques I use to deceive myself but also a matter of accepting your grace. Help me not to reject it. Help me to see that I don't have to make myself big anymore, for I have been anointed a king and a priest just as Saul was, all by your graciousness. Though Saul wasn't affected by this truth, let me be. Let me be liberated by it. In Jesus's name I pray. Amen.

CHAPTER 3

SIN AS LEAVEN

Mark 8:11–17; 7:25–30

Mark 8:11–17

[11] The Pharisees came and began to question Jesus. To test him, they asked him for a sign from heaven. [12] He sighed deeply and said, "Why does this generation ask for a miraculous sign? I tell you the truth, no sign will be given to it." [13] Then he left them, got back into the boat and crossed to the other side.

[14] The disciples had forgotten to bring bread, except for one loaf they had with them in the boat.

¹⁵ "Be careful," Jesus warned them. "Watch out for the yeast of the Pharisees and that of Herod."

¹⁶ They discussed this with one another and said, "It is because we have no bread."

¹⁷ Aware of their discussion, Jesus asked them: "Why are you talking about having no bread? Do you still not see or understand? Are your hearts hardened?

Mark 7:25–30

²⁵ In fact, as soon as she heard about [Jesus], a woman whose little daughter was possessed by an evil spirit came and fell at his feet. ²⁶ The woman was a Greek, born in Syrian Phoenicia. She begged Jesus to drive the demon out of her daughter.

²⁷ "First let the children eat all they want," he told her, "for it is not right to take the children's bread and toss it to their dogs."

²⁸ "Yes, Lord," she replied, "but even the dogs under the table eat the children's crumbs."

²⁹ Then he told her, "For such a reply, you may go; the demon has left your daughter."

³⁰ She went home and found her child lying on the bed, and the demon gone.

One of my favorite poems was written by the seventeenth-century poet George Herbert. It's called "Love (III)," and what truly opened it up for me as I was studying it years ago was understanding how innkeepers in Herbert's time worked.

When a traveler came into an inn hot, tired, and hungry, the first thing the innkeeper did was to inquire what the traveler lacked, what the traveler needed. In this poem, Herbert considers Jesus the innkeeper full of love, and he considers a soul coming to Jesus feeling unworthy and filled with a sense of sin. The first stanza reads,

> Love bade me welcome. Yet my soul drew back
> Guilty of dust and sin.

But quick-eyed Love, observing me grow slack
    From my first entrance in,
Drew nearer to me, sweetly questioning,
    If I lacked any thing.[1]

The rest of the dialogue features the soul claiming it is unworthy to be there and asking to depart in shame. At the end, Jesus the innkeeper says, "Who bore the blame?" He tells the soul to sit down and eat. And the soul does.

This chapter looks at two passages that, like the poem, are about sitting down and eating. They come to us from Mark 8 and 7, two accounts close together in the gospel of Mark in which two sets of seekers come searching for Jesus. In both cases, Jesus talks to them in terms of bread, but these seekers come with greatly different attitudes, as we will see. Those differences, as well as Jesus's responses, teach us something else about sin. In Mark 8 Jesus uses a specific metaphor that vividly illustrates how sin affects us. Jesus compares sin to yeast, or to leaven. Contemporary translations tend to use the word "yeast," while older translations use the word "leaven." Whichever word is used, the metaphor is the same, and Jesus uses the word as a warning: "Watch out for the yeast of the Pharisees" (Mark 8:15).

Why does Jesus call sin leaven, or yeast? What does using that metaphor teach us, and how can we "watch out" for it? First, let's keep in mind that there are a lot of good things about yeast, while there's nothing good about sin. All metaphors fall apart eventually, but here's what the ancients knew about yeast: They knew if you put it into dough—even just a little lump of it—it spreads throughout the mixture. The dough rises, and as long as you bake it soon enough, the bread will be good. But they also understood that the longer the yeast is in the dough, the sourer it becomes. If you leave the dough to set for too long, the yeast sucks all the sweetness out of the loaf and makes it inedible.

Today we know that yeast is a living thing. It's a microorganism that digests the sugar in the dough and breaks it into two parts: alcohol and carbon dioxide. The alcohol evaporates, but the carbon dioxide remains in the bread and makes it rise. However, if you allow the yeast enough time, it takes *all* the sugar out. Yeast will eventually destroy whatever it's in by making it bitter.

Jesus's audience knew this. They knew that yeast works in a hidden way, unseen. They knew it spreads rapidly. And they knew it sucks the sweetness out of bread. And because they understood these characteristics of yeast, they understood Jesus's point: The way yeast works in bread is the way sin works in us.

Sin Hides on the Inside

Ultimately, sin is an unseen, hidden, internal thing. If you saw two bakers making dough, one with leaven and one without, you wouldn't be able to tell which dough was which. What you see externally is no guarantee of what is occurring internally. This is something that Jesus continually tried to get across to the Pharisees, the religious leaders of his day.

The Pharisees were very concerned about external matters: behavior, appearances, and rituals. But again and again, Jesus tried to tell them that sin does its best work in the hidden motives of the heart. It is primarily internal. It is a matter of thoughts and intentions and motives and stances—not just what we can see from the outside.

The difference between sin and grace in the heart is an invisible but utterly distinct disparity of spirit. The spirit of sin says, *Your life for mine.* The spirit of grace says, *My life for yours.* At every moment of the day, we can choose one or the other. To use a minor example, we can choose to cut in line (*Your life for mine.*), or we can choose to let somebody into line ahead of us (*My life for yours.*). Does my spirit believe you exist to serve me or that I exist to serve you?

Like the Pharisees, we can give money to the poor, be sexually pure, go to church all the time, and act morally upright in many other ways and nevertheless operate with the philosophy of *Your life for mine.* And this philosophy, as we will see shortly, will destroy us.

John Owen, a Puritan writer from the seventeenth century, once put it in a spine-tingling way: "Sin is never less quiet than when it seems to be the most quiet, and its waters are for the most part deep when they are still."[2] Just as shallow brooks are noisier and deep streams are quieter, sin is strongest when it's at its quietest.

In other words, sin is most powerful when we don't even see it, when we're not troubled about it, and when we're offended by the idea that we're a sinner in the first place. This is when the predator is most effective—it takes us over from the inside, from the motives of our heart.

Sin Always Spreads

Jesus also tells us that if we do not master our sin, it will spread relentlessly. He uses the metaphor of yeast to make this point. When bakers have leavened dough that has risen, they sometimes pinch off a lump before putting the rest in the oven. The lump becomes the starter for the next loaf of bread. When they make a new batch of dough, they take that earlier lump of leavened bread and mix it in with the new dough. Immediately it works itself in, spreading rapidly.

What is Jesus trying to say through this metaphor? He is warning us that we can't isolate sin in one corner of our heart, expecting it to remain separate, unaffecting other areas of our life.

The principle is this: You might think you can leave sin alone, but sin will never leave *you* alone. Sin is like gangrene. No one with gangrene in their leg thinks, "Well, at least it's just in that one part of my leg. I'll have to limp a little bit, but that will be it." No, they know the choice is either you kill the disease with antibiotics or you cut off the leg, because gangrene always spreads. If you don't kill the gangrene, it will kill you because it never stays sequestered. The same is true of sin. It always spreads. In 1 Corinthians 5:6 the apostle Paul takes up the same metaphor, writing, "Don't you know that a little yeast works through the whole batch of dough?" If Jesus and Paul use the same metaphor, we should pay attention to it.

Let's look at some examples of how this works. Take, for instance, resentment. All of us occasionally have resentful thoughts about someone who has done us wrong. It could be a spouse who hurt us, parents who mistreated us, or a circle of people in our profession who have cost us financially or professionally.

We think something along the lines of, "What an awful person they are. Look at how much they hurt me." In that moment, we have a choice of what to do with the resentful thought: We can fight it, or we can let it live. If we let it live, the thought spreads. Before long, we find ourselves replaying in our head the wrong that was done to us. Then we start actively wishing for the person's downfall or comeuppance. We may even imagine how much better our life would be if they hadn't ever entered it—or even anyone else's. The resentment grows and grows.

The other option is to fight the initial thought, to challenge every motion of it. Whenever we see it cropping up, we root it out. We argue against it instead of letting it spread. We strive to forgive, even when it involves the painful work of stretching our forgiveness beyond what is comfortable.

We must choose one option or the other. There is no leaving the thought alone, because it will not leave us alone. It will take over our whole life if we do not excise it. And when it is good and grown, it will break out. We may antagonize people verbally or even physically. We'll make it our life's mission to hurt the people who hurt us. This is the fruit of a life soured by the sin of resentment. But we won't stop there. We'll identify people who we assume will probably hurt us, if given the chance, and we'll go to war with them as well. But you know what? Those people very well may hurt us now that we've become an unpleasant, cynical person.

This is how sin takes all our sweetness out. It digests all of it and leaves us bitter. Resentment cannot be kept around—it demands a choice: to forgive or perish.

Let me give you another example. Let's say you're married and you have sexual thoughts about someone other than your spouse. You have a choice to fight against that fantasy or indulge in it. If you indulge in it, there's no way to have just *one* fantasy about that person. Having one leads to having more, and those lead to fantasies about other people. Then what's going to happen?

The lust will suck all the sweetness out of your life. You will be drained of the ability to enjoy your spouse. Neither they nor any other human being will be able to live up to your fantasies. You will constantly be chasing an impossible idea, not only mentally but physically. Then it will break out and lead to adultery and unfaithfulness. There is no keeping the fantasy contained; there is no entertaining it without consequences.

We let sin spread like this again and again in different forms. It's no secret that lies multiply like yeast until they run our lives over. And envy demands we go to further and further extremes to get what we want. No matter what form it takes, sin flourishes when ignored.

Sin Is a Proud Denial of Grace

In 1 Corinthians 5, part of which we quoted earlier, Paul says prideful boasting is like leaven. Jesus's run-in with the Pharisees in the passage from Mark evidences this. The Pharisees demand a sign from heaven to prove Jesus is the Messiah. They want a miracle that will convince them.

What does Jesus say? Surprisingly, he says no. What's odd about this response is that Jesus has already performed plenty of miracles. The Pharisees have already seen them. And Jesus goes on to do more miracles after this encounter with them. So why would Jesus say no to their request when he has already *been* doing what they asked?

He refuses their request in order to teach them this: The essence of sin is the proud denial of grace. The reason the Pharisees couldn't believe was not that Jesus hadn't given them any signs. It was because they didn't want what Jesus brought, what Jesus was. They wanted a strong, militant Messiah who would reward them for being pious leaders of Israel. But Jesus had come not as a Messiah of strength but as a Messiah of weakness, a humble teacher.

Jesus performed plenty of miracles, but they were *redemptive* miracles, such as healing people. They weren't revolutionary miracles in the way the Pharisees wanted. He wasn't casting down the Romans. He wasn't taking political and military power and rewarding the religious. He had come as a Messiah of grace to forgive. And the Pharisees didn't see that they needed forgiveness.

Plenty of evidence for Jesus's divine nature existed, but because the Pharisees refused to change their expectations, because they wouldn't acknowledge their need for a Savior, they could not believe. They blamed their unbelief on Jesus and told him it was *his* problem, not theirs. In response, Jesus basically says, "Don't you see? If you deny my idea of grace, you will always ask for more and more signs, and you'll never be satisfied."

Some of us do the same thing. We may think, for example, "Something bad is happening in my life, and if God doesn't come through, I don't know if I'm going to have anything to do with him. He needs to give me a sign and answer my prayer, or I won't believe in him."

But this line of thinking is based on the pharisaic assumption that God owes us. When we deny that we're sinners who deserve nothing from God yet have been given everything when Jesus died for us, we deny the very idea of grace and blame both our problems and our lack of faith on God. When that is the case, no matter how many signs God gives us, we always want another one. If we reject God's grace, we will always be unhappy. We'll always be restless. We must get rid of our stubborn pride and foster an understanding of the Lord's graciousness instead.

Some of you may think, "I'm not proud like those Pharisees. If anything, I'm the opposite of proud of myself. I feel like a failure." God is speaking to you here as well. He is saying, "My Son, Jesus Christ, died on the cross for you. What better sign could you ever have that he loves and accepts you?"

There are two kinds of pride. One kind thinks, "I'm too good for grace." The other thinks, "I'm too bad for grace." People with the first kind of pride reject God's forgiveness because they believe God owes them more signs. People with the second kind reject his forgiveness because they believe they haven't earned it. Both ignore the greatest sign they could ever have: that Christ was crucified to save them.

Years ago a young girl said to me, "Yeah, I'm a Christian, but what good is it if I don't get any dates? Nobody loves me. I feel like killing myself." She was asking God for a sign: *Give me a man who loves me.*

In light of this passage, we can imagine Jesus's response to that girl: "If I gave you a man who loved you, that still wouldn't be enough. You'd want another sign, then another, then another because you have rejected the best sign you could ever have—the one you *already* have. My grace is how you can know you're loved. My grace is how you can know there's hope. There are no better signs I can give than this."

This brings us, finally, to the other passage from Mark at the start of this chapter. The Greek woman depicted here understands God's grace. She comes to Jesus to ask him to drive the demon out of her daughter. Jesus replies, "First let the children eat all they want, . . . for it is not right to take the children's bread and toss it to their dogs" (Mark 7:27). He refers to the fact that he came to earth first for the children of Israel and that the Jews often saw the Greeks as impure and unclean; they were seen as dogs.

What she says in response is the most wonderful example of having faith in God's grace. This is the kind of faith that, if you embrace it in your heart, will spread and undo the problems there. She says, "Yes, Lord, . . . but even the dogs under the table eat the children's crumbs" (v. 28). In other words, "Yes, Lord, I know you came for them. But there are always leftovers for us dogs."

On the one hand, she's admitting that she *is* a dog—that she, like every other human being, is unworthy of the presence of God. But on the other hand, she proclaims that God is too generous to withhold his presence from her. His table is filled with bread. He has more than enough for her.

This woman displays not only a humility that goes against

the proud rejection of grace but also a boldness that says, "I know you're a merciful God. I want what I know you have." Together, those two things—humility and boldness—will heal us. The one thing she didn't know, but we do, is what had to happen to Jesus for her to get the bread.

Jesus had to die for our sins to become the Bread of heaven. He had to be broken in order for there to be plenty for all of us. We can be healed of sin if we see this and say, "This is the one sign I need; I refuse to look for any other sign that God is who he says he is—and that he loves me." Sin is what makes us want something more than this. Pride makes us feel either too good or too bad for this.

Jesus was a living example of the principle *My life for yours.* The more we grasp that he gave his life for us, the more we'll be able to do the same for others.

A PRAYER TO SEE GOD'S GRACE

Father, help me to see that, because of my sin that spreads everywhere, I am infected with a spirit that says, "Your life for mine." But help me also to see that your Son came to give his life for me. I pray you would please allow this ultimate sign of his love to destroy my pride, my fear, and my anxiety. May the reality of Jesus's sacrifice and love become so known to me that I live my life with the same spirit he had: My life for yours. I pray in Jesus's name. Amen.

CHAPTER 4

SIN AS MISTRUST

Jeremiah 17:5–14

[5] This is what the LORD says:
    "Cursed is the one who trusts in man,
        who depends on flesh for his strength
        and whose heart turns away from the LORD.
    [6] He will be like a bush in the wastelands;
        he will not see prosperity when it comes.
    He will dwell in the parched places of the desert,
        in a salt land where no one lives.
    [7] "But blessed is the man who trusts in the LORD,
        whose confidence is in him.

⁸ He will be like a tree planted by the water
    that sends out its roots by the stream.
It does not fear when heat comes;
    its leaves are always green.
It has no worries in a year of drought
    and never fails to bear fruit."
⁹ The heart is deceitful above all things
    and beyond cure.
    Who can understand it?
¹⁰ "I the LORD search the heart
    and examine the mind,
to reward a man according to his conduct,
    according to what his deeds deserve."
¹¹ Like a partridge that hatches eggs it did not lay
    is the man who gain riches by unjust means.
When his life is half gone, they will desert him,
    and in the end he will prove to be a fool.
¹² A glorious throne, exalted from the beginning,
    is the place of our sanctuary.
¹³ O LORD, the hope of Israel;
    all who forsake you will be put to shame.
Those who turn away from you will be written
    in the dust
    because they have forsaken the LORD,
    the spring of living water.
¹⁴ Heal me, O LORD, and I will be healed;
    save me and I will be saved,
    for you are the one I praise.

We all have things we worry about—sociological, psychological, or otherwise. We may be fearful or hateful of certain people groups—a sociological issue. We may grapple with insecurity about our self-image—a psychological issue. We may worry about our finances or our reputation or our family. Whatever the worry is, we often try to fix these things on a surface level. But the Bible says we will never truly deal with them unless we look beneath the surface and see the real source of our problems.

This long passage to the people of Israel from the prophet Jeremiah helps us see the source. In the passage, Jeremiah denounces the people for their sin, and during the denunciation he makes a fascinating comparison of two types of trees that reveals another facet of sin's nature and effects.

We see the comparison in verses 5 to 8. In verse 5 and 6, Jeremiah says that the person "who trusts in man, who depends on flesh for his strength . . . [is] like a bush in the wastelands." Jeremiah then says in verse 7 and 8 that "the man who trusts in the LORD, whose confidence is in him" is like a healthy tree growing next to a river.

Significantly, verse 8 goes further, saying that the tree planted by the river has "no worries." Jeremiah claims to have the secret to dealing with our anxiety and worries. He knows their origin and how to solve them. The picture of the two trees reveals how.

The Root of Sin

The metaphor of the two trees shows us that the essence of sin is *putting our roots into something besides God.* When I've preached or written about sin in the past, every so often someone will reach out to me and say, "You've shown me what sin does and how dangerous it is, but what the heck is it?" Maybe you've wondered the same thing. If so, the good news is that this passage gives us a profound analysis of sin.

The first tree in verse 6 is nothing more than a naked bush. The word *arar* is related to the Hebrew word for "naked," drawing attention to its location in a bare and stripped land.

By contrast, the other tree is flourishing by a river, large and full and green.

The difference between the two trees arises from where their roots are located. It's not even so much that the roots are different; it's the location of the roots that determines everything about the tree—its leaves, its branches, its trunk, everything.

Why is that? Because roots exist to do two things. First, they anchor the tree into the ground so neither the tree nor the soil blows away. Second, the roots draw nutrients and moisture from the soil and absorb them. The nutrients are important for growth, but the moisture, if the roots go deep enough to access it, allows the tree to survive during drought conditions. These two functions are extremely important to remember when we consider the concept of sin. Sin, this passage teaches us, is planting our roots in something other than God. We often think of sin as something different: a violation of rules. One of the problems with thinking of sin solely in that way is that it causes us to see both sin and godliness as lying on a spectrum. In that view, you could say that a person with fifty violations against God's law is a sinner while a person with three violations is a godly person. And someone with twenty-five violations falls somewhere in the middle.

But Jeremiah tells us we can't see sin this way. We can't say, "Here's a person who's half as good as this other person." Sin and godliness are two different orientations of the heart, two different locations of our roots. We either put our roots down in God or in something else, and where we place them determines everything else about us.

What do I mean by "put our roots down"? The key word in the passage that explains this is "trust." Look at the contrast between verses 5 and 7: "Cursed is the one who *trusts* in man," but "blessed is the man who *trusts* in the LORD." What we trust is where we are rooted. And our roots and our faith are one and the same. Therefore, the person who thinks themselves religious but doesn't functionally, in practice, place their trust and hope in Christ doesn't actually have their roots in God at all.

Some will read this and think, "If faith is what it takes to get rid of sin, I don't know if I'm up to that. I'm not a person of great faith like those other religious people." This line of thinking is a deceit of the heart. Everyone has faith in *something*. To live our lives, we *must* place our trust somewhere, and the course of everything we do is determined by where we put that trust. *Everybody* has faith, just like every tree has roots. Everybody puts their roots down into something for support.

Do you want to find out where your roots are? Let me give you a couple of tests. One is what I call the negative test, and the other is the positive. The negative test asks you a few questions:

- What do you worry about most?
- What scares you most?

- What, if you lost it, would make you feel like your life was crumbling? What would make you feel like you didn't have any substance anymore, or that your life wouldn't be worth living?

Everybody has answers to these questions. What are yours? Whatever they are, they should give you a good idea of what your faith is in, of where your roots lie.

The English bishop William Temple is often said to have phrased the positive test like this: "Religion is what you do with your solitude." When you're not busy with anything—when you don't have to think about your work or your responsibilities or anything else—where does your mind go to get refreshed? What does your mind try to draw nutrients from? Where do you go to get joy? Where do you turn for consolation?

There are plenty of material things our minds may rely on to feel good. We may think of our home, our decorations, our car, our clothes, the next meal we're going to eat, or our television. Or our minds may incline toward relationships. Maybe it's the idea of the perfect romance or the thought of having the perfect family. Maybe you tell yourself, "As long as I've got a big group of friends, I'll be fine." Maybe you even put your hope in the idea of "saving" somebody you think needs you.

Perhaps you reflect on achievements to gain consolation. It could be advancing in your career, investing effort into a political or social cause, mastering a hobby, climbing a mountain, or realizing any of the other goals you've set for yourself.

Whatever your mind draws hope from, *that* is your religion. It's your ultimate concern. This is what you existentially rest in—what makes you feel as if you have substance. Whether you see yourself as a religious person or an irreligious person or somewhere in between makes no difference. Your faith is in something.

In an oft quoted story about Winston Churchill, the prime minister had a spat with his manservant. Afterward, the valet approached Churchill and tried to make up. He admitted he had been rude, then tentatively added, "You know, Mr. Churchill, you were rude to me, too." In all seriousness, Churchill replied, "Yes, but I am a great man."[1]

With that answer, he showed where he planted his roots. When the pressure came, where did he go to justify and restore himself? He looked to his achievements, and his heart responded, "Look at what I've done. So what if I'm spiteful to my valet?"

This is why sin is not simply breaking rules; sin is making something other than God our biggest delight, our existential rest, and our ultimate trust.

This truth is seen throughout the Bible. Psalm 37:4 says, "Delight yourself in the Lord and he will give you the desires of your heart." If our delight is in God, we will flourish. In Matthew 22, when the Pharisees ask Jesus what the greatest commandment in the law is, he answers, "Love the Lord your God with all your heart and with all your soul and with all your mind" (v. 37). That's the sum of what we are to do.

Let me show you how radical of an analysis of sin this passage from Jeremiah is. He goes so far as to say in 17:7, "But blessed is the man who trusts in the LORD, whose confidence is in him." Why does he add that second clause? The English translation masks how powerful this statement is. In the original phrasing, the same Hebrew root is used for the English translation of both "trust" *and* "confidence" here. It's really saying, "Blessed is the man who trusts in the Lord, whose trust *is* the Lord." Why would it need to read like that? Because it's possible to trust in the Lord without making the Lord our trust. Let me explain.

In a sense, there are three kinds of people. First, there is the irreligious person, whose underlying attitude is *I'm going to live life my own way.* Then there is the religious person who does the things God asks but does them to get something from God. That person is trusting in the Lord *for something else*—which means their real trust is in that *something else.* The third person puts their trust in the Lord, and their trust *is* the Lord.

The view of the second person is worth exploring. It's easy to miss what's going on, but we can see it more clearly when something goes wrong in the life of that person. When that occurs, the person thinks, "I've been pretty good. I've been obeying God. And yet he isn't fixing this problem. I'm just asking what any human being would ask, and God isn't coming through for me. I don't know whether I'm going to keep following him. What good is it to be with God? What profit is there?"

This is the view of someone who trusts in the Lord and yet does not make *him* their trust. If anything is a condition for faith in God, then that condition is the real object of faith rather than the Lord. If you think, "I'll trust in God, but if he doesn't come through here, what good is it to be a Christian?," do you know what you have revealed about yourself? You may be trusting in the Lord in some sense, but he's not your *real* trust. Whatever it is you want him to provide is your *real* trust, your *real* hope.

Verse 9 tells us, "The heart is deceitful above all things." We may think we trust God, but we can fool ourselves. Sin is making God a means to an end instead of being the end itself. Sin is making the happy ending you're after more important than an eternal relationship with God himself. If you find yourself saying, "I'm ready to give up on God. Why won't he give me this thing?," what you're really saying is, "This thing, not God, is my trust." If that's the case, why on earth would he give you that thing, when anything you put your roots down into except him will make you twisted and stunted and thirsty? Would that be kind or loving of him?

The Fruit of Sin

This passage contains another comparison between the two trees that doesn't quite come across in this translation. The comparison reveals something about the consequences of sin, about what its fruits are and are not. Verse 6 compares the person whose trust is in man to "a bush in the wastelands; he will not see prosperity when it comes." Shortly after, verse 8 declares that the one who trusts God "will be like a tree planted by the water that sends out its roots by the stream. It does not fear when heat comes." It's a striking contrast. But what is it getting at? It's getting at a difference in how people respond to their circumstances.

How does this work? The bush can't receive the good, the "prosperity," because it has prepared itself to live in the desert. Occasionally, deserts do have downpours, and rain does come, but that doesn't fundamentally change the bush. The rain may make it a little greener for a moment, but it doesn't actually change it. It's still a tree that has adapted to a barren environment.

Conversely, the tree by the river may go through a desert-like drought, but that also will not fundamentally change the tree. The season may affect it to some degree, sure—its leaves may be a little browner for a time—but it will not die from lack of rain. The true source of its moisture is the river, not the weather. As a result, drought doesn't make the tree any less vital, just as a downpour doesn't really transform the desert tree.

What is this metaphor getting at? Some people who would like to make money get rich. Some who want to garner achievements become famous. Some who desire a romantic relationship get exactly what they want. They find themselves in a downpour. Prosperity comes. But it will be one of the worst things for them.

Years ago in *The Village Voice*, the alternative newspaper based in New York City, Cynthia Heimel wrote an article called "The Celebrity Decade" in which she talks about our cultural obsession with celebrity, the desire for fame—and the awfulness of getting it. She notes that of the thousands who "fervently . . . wanted fame," only a few achieved it. And those who did were desperately unhappy:

> The morning after each of them became famous they wanted to take an overdose . . . because that giant thing they were striving for, that fame thing that was going to make everything OK, that was going to make their lives bearable, that was going to provide them with personal fulfillment and (ha ha) happiness had happened. And nothing changed. And they were still them. The disillusionment turned them howling and insufferable.[2]

This is exactly what Jeremiah says. A downpour in the desert is temporary; it will still leave you thirsty if your roots are not planted by the stream. If they aren't, finally getting your rain is one of the worst experiences you can have because it's not going to save you. And you will be left "howling and insufferable."

On the other hand, Jeremiah tells us, the person whose roots are in God can weather dry seasons. If bad things happen to them, their attitude is *I may be disappointed, but these aren't the main things I need. God is who I really want.* As a result, they experience these things without fear or worry.

This is the way we need to look at our lives. When we look at the weather—at our circumstances—and think, "All of my problems are because it's not raining. If only I had the right wife," or "If only I had the right husband," or "If only I had a job or a new job," we aren't seeing that these things won't ultimately satisfy us. The crucial thing is not what "precipitation" we receive or whether we're a little green or a little brown at any moment, but whether we are near the river. If we're worried, if we're afraid, if we're anxious about something, what does that tell us? Not just that we're beleaguered by our circumstances. It reveals where our trust is truly placed.

We have to be willing to look at whatever our trust is in (and it may be a good thing) and say to ourselves, "I have my roots in that. *That's* why I'm worried. My roots aren't near the river of God."

This is an incredibly convicting practice, but also a very liberating one. When we realize we are not victims of our circumstances but sinners who can call on someone much greater than ourselves to care for us, we can begin to truly live.

In this passage in Jeremiah, it's as if God is speaking to our hearts, saying, "Think about it. What do you really want out of love and sex? You want closure. You want commitment.

Well, know me. What do you really want out of your career? You want significance. You want to feel like you've made a difference. Serve me. What do you want from money? You want security and happiness. Trust me."

What is a raindrop to a river?

The Cure for Sin

So, what is the cure for our mistrust? Verse 14 starts with Jeremiah saying, "Heal me, O LORD." What is it that needs healing? Our hearts. Verse 9 tells us, "The heart is deceitful above all things and beyond cure." Jeremiah says the heart's sin is incurable, and yet five verses later he tells God, "Heal me." Is he contradicting himself? Not in the least.

What he's saying is actually simple: Our hearts are incurable by *humans*. If you look carefully, you'll see that verse 6 tells us that the desert bush is simply "in the wastelands," but by contrast the second tree is "planted by the water" (v. 8). Why would Jeremiah say it's planted? Because we are desert trees by nature, cropping up in the wilds. But we can't simply get up and plant ourselves elsewhere. We need to be planted. We need outside intervention to experience rebirth.

To be placed by the river of God, we must let the God of the river take us up and plant us himself.

If you find yourself wondering, "How do I know if I need to be replanted?," observe how well you do in a drought.

When the heat comes, are you able to deal with it? Either you will weather it, or it will dry you up, cause you to feel as if you're dying, or even turn you "howling and insufferable."

Have you ever had a spiritual turning point in your life? Have you ever felt God pulling your roots out of the old things and putting them into the new? Have you ever experienced spiritual struggle? Or are you thinking, "No, I've always been a pretty good person. I've always gone to church. I've always believed"? If those are your thoughts, that's a very bad sign.

If you haven't experienced being replanted, you need God's regeneration.

There are some who would say that, sure, the things of this life will leave us disappointed and broken—but becoming a Christian won't fix that. Religion, too, will leave us just as disillusioned as everything else, they say. My reply would be that if you think Christianity is too weak to give you real hope—if you think you're okay without God—you haven't really experienced the heat.

What if someday a doctor comes to you and says, "I have bad news. Pretty soon you'll be in a wheelchair for the rest of your life." No more career, no more financial security, no more sex, no more walking around on your own two feet.

What soil could possibly give you enough nutrients to make it through such a diagnosis? The hope of Christ will. Christianity gives you the resources for the vision and the courage to face something like that. With roots in God, you can still experience love. You can still have significance.

You can know that, regardless of what your body does or doesn't do, you are part of the most important cosmic drama ever to unfold. When properly planted, Christians are the exact opposite of weak people; they are the only people who can face anything at all.

If all this is true, the question is, How can we be replanted? First, we must become convicted of sin. The best way to do this is to look at its definition, to remember its essence: making something other than God our biggest delight, our existential rest, and our ultimate trust. Don't tell yourself, "Well, I'm a pretty good person." Ask yourself, "Do I love God with all my heart, soul, strength, and mind? Do I delight in him utterly?"

If God is the source of all glory and goodness, all beauty and harmony—and he is—then of course we should love him above everything else. But we don't. In fact, we utterly fail. So if you understand the definition of sin, you will see your need. You will see you are a failure, as every human is, and then you can turn to God as Jeremiah did and say, "Heal me."

How exactly can he heal us? What—or who—makes God's healing possible? Throughout the history of the world, many people who have been thirsty and spiritually shriveled have been plucked out of the desert and planted by the river of God. In his grace, God has done it for many of us. But only one person in history started next to the river and was uprooted to be thrown into the desert. Only one.

Why did Satan tempt Jesus Christ after he was alone in

the desert? It was boot camp for what Jesus was going to go through. When he was on the cross, what did he say? He said, "I am thirsty" (John 19:28). The crucifixion was the real desert. Up until that point, he had known only the river of God and his favor and love.

But on the cross Jesus's soul dried up, crumbled into a million pieces, and was blown away. He was forsaken; he forfeited the river so that we may be allowed into it.

Many Christians reading this may be thinking, "You know, I've heard this before. This chapter isn't really for me. I'm already planted by the river." If you think that, please think about this: Are you still worried? Are you ever distressed?

In the first two chapters of the book of Job, God and Satan have an argument about Job, a servant of God who enjoys a good life. Satan challenges God by asking, "Does Job fear God for nothing?" (Job 1:9). Satan implies that Job trusts in the Lord, but that Job's trust is *not* the Lord. If his blessings are taken away, Satan believes, Job will curse God and reveal himself as a halfhearted follower. But through all the troubles God allows to come into Job's life, we see that he is not a hypocrite. Job is a believer. He is planted by the river— but even he needs to be planted closer. Many Christians are by the river but need to be a lot closer as well. Any disillusion or worries in our life remain because of that fact. So what do we do to turn our roots more toward the river?

In Ephesians 3:17–19, Paul prays for the Ephesians, "I

pray that you, being rooted and established in love, may have power, together with all the saints [which just means those who belong to him], to grasp how wide and long and high and deep is the love of Christ, and to know this love that surpasses knowledge—that you may be filled to the measure of all the fullness of God." Those verses describe a discipline, a process. Christians aren't finished growing simply because they've seen or heard about the love of God. Paul is praying that they would have *communion* with the love of God—that their roots would grow closer to that river.

Years ago I was meditating in prayer about how Jesus thirsted. I thought about him leaving the river and being tossed into the desert. As I was meditating, I felt something I can't summon simply by my own will. Thanks to God and his graciousness, I felt a flood of his love in that moment, like I could face anything.

When we think about Jesus's thirst, it's the end of ours. We must take the time daily to meditate on his substitution of himself to pay for our sin, otherwise we will dry up. Our roots won't be receiving the nourishment and hydration they need. When I first preached this chapter as a sermon, I woke up scared. I wasn't prepared. I thought, "What's the matter with me?" My anxiety was because I hadn't taken the time that week to return my roots to the river.

I know you get worried, because I get worried. I know you're often scared, because I often get scared. But God offers us a way out. By being rooted and grounded in love, looking at Christ's thirst until ours goes away, meditating on what he has done and communing with him, and making the Lord our trust, we can experience true peace, true forgiveness, and the loving care of the one true God. As Jesus said in John 7:38, "Whoever believes in me, as the Scripture has said, streams of living water will flow from within him." This is how we become planted by the river, enabling us to face without worry whatever drought comes our way.

A PRAYER TO BE ROOTED IN GOD

Our Father, I ask you to help me see what it is you're call-ing me to. If I need the rebirth of being replanted, may I seek you for it. Help me say, "Heal me, Lord, and I will be healed; save me and I will be saved, for you are the one I praise."

Father, forgive me for often neglecting to make you my trust. Because I don't praise you like I should, I am not as healed as I could be. Let me remember this and be changed through applying this truth to my heart by the Spirit. May I feel my anxiety and worry wash away as you replant me close to your stream and I place my faith in you and what Christ has done for me. I pray in Jesus's name. Amen.

CHAPTER 5

SIN AS
SELF-RIGHTEOUSNESS

Jonah 2:1–2, 7–3:5; 3:10–4:11

2:1 From inside the fish Jonah prayed to the
LORD his God. 2 He said: . . .
⁷"When my life was ebbing away,
   I remembered you, LORD,
and my prayer rose to you,
   to your holy temple.
⁸"Those who cling to worthless idols
   forfeit the grace that could be theirs.

⁹ But I, with a song of thanksgiving,
     will sacrifice to you.
What I have vowed I will make good.
     Salvation comes from the LORD."

¹⁰ And the LORD commanded the fish, and it vomited Jonah onto dry land.

³:¹ Then the word of the LORD came to Jonah a second time: ² "Go to the great city of Nineveh and proclaim to it the message I give you."

³ Jonah obeyed the word of the LORD and went to Nineveh. Now Nineveh was a very important city—a visit required three days. ⁴ On the first day, Jonah started into the city. He proclaimed: "Forty more days and Nineveh will be overturned." ⁵ The Ninevites believed God. They declared a fast, and all of them, from the greatest to the least, put on sackcloth. . . .

¹⁰ When God saw what they did and how they turned from their evil ways, he had compassion and did not bring upon them the destruction he had threatened.

⁴:¹ But Jonah was greatly displeased and became angry. ² He prayed to the LORD, "O LORD, is this not what I said when I was still at home? That is why I was so quick to flee to Tarshish. I knew that you are a gracious and compassionate God, slow to anger and

abounding in love, a God who relents from sending calamity. ³ Now, O LORD, take away my life, for it is better for me to die than to live."

⁴ But the LORD replied, "Have you any right to be angry?"

⁵ Jonah went out and sat down at a place east of the city. There he made himself a shelter, sat in its shade and waited to see what would happen to the city. ⁶ Then the LORD God provided a vine and made it grow up over Jonah to give shade for his head to ease his discomfort, and Jonah was very happy about the vine. ⁷ But at dawn the next day God provided a worm, which chewed the vine so that it withered. ⁸ When the sun rose, God provided a scorching east wind, and the sun blazed on Jonah's head so that he grew faint. He wanted to die, and said, "It would be better for me to die than to live."

⁹ But God said to Jonah, "Do you have a right to be angry about the vine?"

"I do," he said. "I am angry enough to die."

¹⁰ But the LORD said, "You have been concerned about this vine, though you did not tend it or make it grow. It sprang up overnight and died overnight. ¹¹ But Nineveh has more than a hundred and twenty thousand people who cannot tell their right hand from their left, and many cattle as well. Should I not be concerned about that great city?"

In previous chapters, we explored how sin is a stance of the heart before it's a matter of behavior. The message of the book of Jonah gives us a concrete example of that reality. The first part of the book of Jonah is famous, so famous I've not reprinted it here. But the rest of the story is not nearly as well known, despite it being arguably more important. We'll closely examine the second part in this chapter, but here's a reminder of what happens at the beginning of the book. God calls Jonah to go to Nineveh: "Go to the great city of Nineveh and preach against it, because its wickedness has come up before me" (Jonah 1:2).

Jonah, however, runs away. He tries to flee from the

Lord by chartering a ship to Tarshish, heading in the opposite direction of where he was called to go. *The Jesus Storybook Bible* by Sally Lloyd-Jones offers an amusing illustration of this part of the story: Jonah standing in front of two road markers, one pointing to "Nineveh" and the other pointing to "Not Nineveh." Jonah's destination was anywhere but where he was being sent.

Most people know what happens next: As Jonah is trying to get away, God sends a storm of his anger, and when the boat is on the verge of being torn apart, Jonah says to the sailors, "Pick me up and throw me into the sea . . . and it will become calm. I know that it is my fault that this great storm has come upon you" (Jonah 1:12). They do as he says, and Jonah is swallowed by a huge fish.

In the fish, he comes to his senses and humbles himself, praying the prayer found at the beginning of this chapter. What happens then is deeply revealing about the nature of sin.

Jonah was a religious leader, a moral, theologically orthodox man who was nevertheless, in the end, more a slave to sin than the debauched pagans to whom he was sent. This is what makes Jonah's story so important in revealing the nature and danger of sin. If we do not understand the essential spirit of sin—that a very religious, seemingly moral person can be just as bound by it as an irreligious or skeptical person—then sin stands a good chance of defeating us.

What else does Jonah's story teach us about sin? First, we see that God goes to Jonah and shows him the *symptoms* of his sin, giving him two signs that his heart is morally disordered. Then he provides Jonah the *diagnosis* of his sin. Finally, we see *God's therapy* for sin.

The Symptoms of Jonah's Sin

God points out two signs that something is wrong with Jonah. The first thing he points out is that Jonah doesn't care about anyone in Nineveh. In verses 10 and 11 of chapter 4, God asks him why, if he is so concerned with the plant that gave him shade, does he have no concern for the 120,000 people who live in the city?

The Hebrew word translated "concerned" in verses 10 and 11 is difficult to fully explain in English, but we can begin by noting that it implies to both love something and grieve or have pity over it. Jonah, of course, does not have such an attitude toward the people of Nineveh. God tells him to look inside himself and ask why. Why doesn't he have the love for the people of the city that God has? Why does he have more love for a single plant than for thousands of people and animals?

In the very beginning of the book, God says to Jonah, "Go to the great city of Nineveh and preach against it, because its wickedness has come up before me" (Jonah 1:2). God wants him to go because Nineveh is becoming more broken. It's growing more violent. Things are getting worse there.

When Jonah decides not to go to Nineveh, he may have rationalized his decision (and deceived himself) by thinking, "Nineveh is a dangerous place. If I go there and preach about God's destruction, I could be destroyed myself."

But by chapter 4, all the danger is gone. The city has listened to Jonah, and now he can't hide the original reason he ran: he hates those filthy, creepy pagans. He didn't want to see God do anything good to them; he has no concern for them. When God comes to him and asks him how he could fail to love the city, God's question reveals that there's something wrong with Jonah's heart.

Jonah's feelings toward Nineveh are like those of most believers who see a similar situation and think, "I'm leaving the city because it's getting worse every day. This place is only getting more and more violent and further away from God. I'm getting out of here." This response may seem logical when we think of the inconveniences and dangers of living in a city, but when it comes to God's global mission, it's illogical. If the goal is to spread the news of Christ as far as we can and reach as many people as possible, where would it be more necessary for God's people to live than a city full of people who need the gospel? The worse it gets, the more reason we have to go there.

Are your mind's logic and your heart's attitude toward the city more like Jonah's or God's? As God's own words here reveal, it doesn't make sense for a Christian to witness a city full of people who need God and care nothing about them. Shouldn't we be filled with love for the lost?

This is what the plant in chapter 4 makes clear. Anyone who has ever gardened knows how attached you can get to a plant. When we see something that we love destroyed, we grow unhappy. This is normal, of course. But God points out that Jonah is more grieved over a single ruined plant than thousands of ruined lives. That makes no logical sense. Jonah's heart is behaving irrationally. This is his first symptom of sin.

Jonah's second symptom is his anger. God appears to Jonah on two separate occasions to point this out to him. In both verses 4 and 9 of chapter 4, he asks, "Have you any right to be angry?" The second time, Jonah answers, "I do. . . . I am angry enough to die." He is so bitter in his soul that he has lost all desire to live. God soon corrects this outrage.

Allow me to issue two disclaimers. First, this does not mean that anger itself is necessarily a sin. Sometimes anger is just. God gets very angry. Jesus got angry while he was on earth. The issue here is not the anger per se.

Second, despair of life is not necessarily a sin either. Job, for example, was in utter agony and tremendous physical pain. In such a circumstance, saying "I would like to die" is an understandable response. There are also physiological, chemical, and hormonal reasons why a person can sink into depression. But that's not the case here.

Jonah's circumstances are different. Both his anger and despair are fruits of his sin. God points out that they are disproportionate to what he's experiencing. Why is he *trapped* in his anger? Why has he been sapped of all the desire to live? Understanding the answer to these questions will reveal much about the nature of Jonah's sin.

The Diagnosis of Jonah's Sin

Like a good counselor, God puts Jonah into the position where Jonah himself identifies the diagnosis for his symptoms, though he doesn't seem to realize it. After God spares the city, Jonah says in 4:2, "Is this not what I said when I was still at home? That is why I was so quick to flee to Tarshish. I knew that you are a gracious and compassionate God, slow to anger and abounding in love, a God who relents from sending calamity." In other words, he's saying, "This is the reason I didn't want to come to begin with. This is the reason I'm devastated. I knew you are a God of graciousness."

That word "gracious" is translated from the Hebrew word *chesed*, which refers to God's saving love. Jonah says that what's bothering him is that God is giving his saving love not just to the righteous, religious people of Israel but to their enemies—those dirty pagans—as well. These pagans were growing in such power that they may have destroyed Israel if they weren't destroyed themselves first. It is offensive to Jonah that these people could ever be offered the same salvation he has.

What this reveals is that the heart of sin is self-righteousness. When we think of the word *righteous* today, we usually take it to mean someone moral, pious, and probably quite holier-than-thou. But the Bible does not use the word in such a negative way. In fact, it teaches us that *everyone* seeks righteousness. Why? Because righteousness is the opposite of shame. We want to be right!

To seek righteousness means we look at something and think, "This will make me right. This makes me somebody. This gives me meaning. This gives me confidence." Of course, God is the only one who can truly provide these things. And yet we all take something besides God—it can be good or bad—and make that our confidence, our glory, and our righteousness. Jonah looked to his status as a Hebrew, the one who had the "true God." He did, in fact, worship the true God, but he used that for his own self-image. He was self-righteous.

In Jonah's mind, he was living his life exactly as he should. He was doing all the right things. He thought those actions and beliefs were what gave him meaning, but he was valuing them incorrectly. For example, it's a good thing to be a patriot. It's a good thing to love your people. It was a good thing for him to have pride that, as an Israelite, he knew the Word of God, he followed God, and God had given him his favor. But he idolized this perception of himself so much that when he saw another group of people getting God's favor, he lost his hope. He fell into despair, angry enough to die.

If you feel like nothing after you lose something, it means that the thing you lost was your everything. It was your functional salvation. The reason Jonah is suicidal here is because he has experienced psychological disintegration. His entire self-image was based on feeling morally superior to other cultures and to other religions.

Notice something else: The book of Jonah ends abruptly, oddly. It concludes with God trying to reclaim Jonah and help him see his sin—and it does so with a question.

Why would the book end like that? Because the story is trying to make a point: We're all Jonah. God isn't asking just Jonah these questions; he's asking *all of us* these questions.

We have the same problems that Jonah does. What's wrong with our hearts? We may not all be racists the way Jonah was. We may not turn the national interest of our country into an idol. But we are all deeply self-righteous, wherever we get that righteousness from.

Years ago I read a sermon by George Whitefield that reshaped the way I preach and minister and think about my life. It's called "The Method of Grace," and in it, Whitefield says there are two things you need to do to be a Christian. First, you have to repent of your sin. But that alone isn't enough, because even the Pharisees did that. In addition, you have to repent of your righteousness.

Whitefield says self-righteousness is the "last idol taken out of [your] heart" before you can become a Christian. "The pride of [your] heart will not let [you] submit to the righteousness of Jesus Christ." What he goes on to say in the sermon is that you aren't a Christian until you realize we try to become our own saviors through our disobedience to God *and* our obedience to God.[1]

If you don't recognize your tendency to try to save yourself by obeying the rules and relying on your own righteousness, the effort to become a Christian will stay half finished. You'll repent of your sins year after year after year, but nothing will ever seem to click. You will never seem to really know God, and your heart will remain full of anger and despair, just like Jonah's.

We must remember that salvation comes utterly from the Lord. At the end of chapter 2, Jonah seems to understand this. Before God frees him from the belly of the fish, he proclaims, "Those who cling to worthless idols forfeit the grace that could be theirs" (v. 8). In this moment, he got it. He saw that God's grace was as much for foreign idol worshipers as it was for the Israelites. The lowest person in the gutters of Nineveh was no more lost than the most upstanding citizen in Jerusalem. Through religion or irreligion, from obedience to disobedience, we all resist God as Savior and Lord. We all fall short and have to be saved strictly by grace.

Even though Jonah came to realize all of this, he soon forgot it. The message of Jonah is that to get out of the fish and become a true Christian, we have to acknowledge our self-righteousness and place our hope in God instead. We have to say, "Lord, save me strictly out of grace for Jesus's sake." Yet we continually forget this.

Despite our best efforts, our hearts will often be divided and full of something else we're serving alongside God in the hopes that it will save us. For us to grow as Christians, God must keep showing us new ways in which we have failed to see our self-righteousness. We must open our eyes to see it still operating within us. How can we do this? Look at Jonah's signs of self-righteousness, and apply the standard to yourself. Here are three of his signs.

The first is a sign we've already seen: losing our happiness and will to live when we lose something other than God. In the film *Chariots of Fire*, Harold Abrahams explains his motivation for training to become a sprinter in the Olympics by saying he has "ten lonely seconds to justify my whole existence."[2] In his mind, if he won a gold medal, he would finally matter as a person.

You may not say it as openly as Abrahams, but if you do not understand that you're training for your own sprint to save yourself, you don't know your own heart.

Many years ago one woman put it to me like this: Anything you add to Jesus Christ as a requirement for being happy will strangle you like it strangled Jonah. It will lead to emotional ups and downs, pulling you all over the map as you try to serve it—even making you angry enough to die if you lose it. But you cannot serve two masters.

The second sign of self-righteousness is that we are not a comfort to hurting people, just as Jonah wasn't. When we find ourselves close to those in suffering, we have no hope for them, and we even have a sense of superiority over them. This attitude is very, very important for Christians to be aware of, especially those of us who live in cities.

When I first moved to New York City, a woman came and told me she wasn't a Christian, and as far as I know, she never became one. But she had talked to Christians before. She was a $1,000-a-night prostitute, and whenever she told this to Christians, at the very best, they reacted with a hopeless, stunned silence. They didn't have anything hopeful to say. At the very worst, she could tell that they felt superior to her. They wondered, "How could anyone do such a thing?"

Many Christians who move to places like New York City come from nice, middle-class backgrounds, and when they talk to somebody like this woman and feel only hopelessness, discomfort, disgust, or superiority, do you know what that means? They don't see themselves as a miracle of grace. In instances like this, we may *say* we're a sinner saved by grace, but we don't truly see it as a miracle that God deigned to save someone as sinful as us.

Whether we do so explicitly or implicitly, we're saying to those people, "I'm a Christian, but you and all your baggage are another thing entirely." But no, they're not another thing. That's what God was trying to show Jonah.

Christians have to interact with the world at large just as Jonah did. We need people like the Ninevites to show us our self-righteousness and pharisaic attitudes. Just as they had to teach Jonah about grace before he could say anything to *them* about grace, we need places like Nineveh to show us the gospel before we can ever show *them* the gospel.

But if we remain self-righteous, troubled people will not want to talk to us about their problems because they would feel hopeless at best and looked down upon at worst. God says to Jonah and us that if we understand who we are and what we've done and what we are now through the miraculous gospel of grace, we will never see people's troubles as too vast to impede the grace of God.

God loves the hard cases. God comes down to meet people like us. He chooses the foolish to shame the wise. He chooses the despised to shame the proud. He chooses the weak to shame the strong. That's the reason why he sees the Ninevites and his heart goes crazy with love. Despite their wickedness, he sees all kinds of people whose lives he wants to save—people he wants to do something incredible with. If we can't talk to the hurting people around us with that same kind of hope and with humble respect, we're self-righteous.

Lastly, the most important sign of self-righteousness is that we don't think we're self-righteous. The more self-righteous we know ourselves to be, the less we actually are. The less self-righteous we think ourselves to be, the more we actually are.

If you don't think you're self-righteous at all, you are completely under its control. You may even look back and say, "When I was in the fish (or whatever difficult circumstances you were in), I understood it. Now I've forgotten it."

A Christian has to see their heart as a fountainhead of self-righteousness that flows forth all day, all the time.

For example, why is it we often can't stand to take criticism? Why does it discourage us so much? Because criticism destroys our image of ourselves, and that is often what we build our righteousness on, that makes us unhappy about criticism. By the same token, if we criticize others and they feel attacked by us, this can be a result of our self-righteousness too, because if we think ourselves superior, we will not offer correction in a humble way. In fact, even the desire to criticize can be from self-righteousness. Our motivation may be an irritable insistence that *nobody gets things right but me.*

Self-righteousness is something we need to continually be aware of. Christians are to watch for it all the time, everywhere, at the root of everything—the problem underneath all the things we do. The more we see it, the less it controls us, while the less we see it, the more it controls us.

God's Therapy for Jonah's Sin

The cure for our self-righteousness is the grace of God, of course—we need to recognize that salvation comes from him. This is something that no other religion on the face of the earth says. No other religion says that the lowest person in the gutter and the most moral, upstanding citizen in the world are equally lost, equally need to be saved by grace, and can only be saved by grace alone. These revelations are utterly devastating for self-righteousness. How does God administer this cure of grace to us? First, he applies it *continually*. Second, he applies it *painfully*. Third, he applies it *lovingly*.

First, he applies it continually. Throughout our lives, God keeps coming back to us. God continually has to get our attention and tell us that, once again, we have forgotten the gospel. Over and over, that's the story of the Christian life. *I remembered it in the fish, and then I forgot it at the vine. Then I understood it at the vine.*

How do we know Jonah remembered it at the vine? How do we know that God's final question to him in the story brought him to his senses? Because we have the book of Jonah, and only a Christian, only a person who knows he's saved by grace, would tell a story that makes him look this bad. But I can also say with certainty that if he understood it at the vine, he forgot it later. God repeatedly has to come back to us and remind us, day in and day out.

God has to say to us, in essence, "The reason you're bored, the reason you're defensive, the reason you're scared, the reason you're bitter, the reason you're attacking others, the reason you're fleeing is because you are trying to make something your savior when only I can be your Savior. You're making something besides me your wisdom, your righteousness, your sanctification, and your redemption." He will tell us this again and again and again. And he will never tire of doing so.

Second, God administers his cure painfully. For Jonah, God takes away something he loves: the vine. Sometimes the only possible way for us to understand the shape of our self-righteousness is by having the things we depend on taken away.

In the King James Version, the vine is called a "gourd," and we're told God sent an east wind to blast it to pieces after the worm had eaten it. The eighteenth-century English cleric John Newton wrote a hymn referring to this called "I Asked the Lord That I Might Grow." In it, Newton describes how he asked God to help him grow and become more like him. Then, quite suddenly, everything begins to go wrong in his life:

> Yea more, with His own hand He seemed
> Intent to aggravate my woe;
> Crossed all the fair designs I schemed,
> Blasted my gourds, and laid me low.
>
> Lord, why is this, I trembling cried,
> Wilt thou pursue thy worm to death?
> "'Tis in this way," the Lord replied,
> "I answer prayer for grace and faith.
>
> These inward trials I employ,
> From self and pride to set thee free;
> And break thy schemes of earthly joy,
> That thou may'st find thy all in Me."

Finally, God administers grace lovingly. Notice how when God counsels Jonah, there isn't an ounce of anger. In fact, he counsels Jonah kindly, asking questions gently: "Do you have a right to be angry?" When you ask a person questions, you do so because your focus is on helping them toward the proper solution rather than simply being confrontational.

But why isn't God furious? After all, he did send a storm of his anger while Jonah was on the ship to Tarshish. Here's the answer. Many years later someone stood before a bunch of self-righteous Pharisees and said, "The men of Nineveh will stand up at the judgment with this generation and condemn it; for they repented at the preaching of Jonah, and now one greater than Jonah is here" (Matthew 12:41). The Pharisees had asked Jesus for a sign that he was the Messiah. Jesus replied that no sign would be given to them except the sign of Jonah.

Jesus was saying that just as Jonah was thrown into the representational storm of God's wrath and saved the men in the boat as a result, so he himself would be thrown into the real storm of God's wrath. Jesus was thrown into the real storm of justice as a penalty for sin. He went down to the true depths of the universe. He was utterly crushed and as a result saved everyone in the boat.

The message of Jesus is this: If you come to God through him and say, "Give me your grace," there is no anger for you. Jesus, the one greater than Jonah, is here. He was thrown into the storm so God could come to us and gently say, in effect, "When will you see the grace I have for you? Let me show you how you can be truly free through my love." This is what he did for Jonah, administering grace as a cure for his sin. And this is what he can do for you.

A PRAYER FOR HEALING FROM
SELF-RIGHTEOUSNESS

Our Father, I know your table is not for people who think they're righteous; it's for those who know they're sinners. Now enable me to come and sit down with you, hear your gentle questions, and forsake my self-righteousness so I too can live a life of freedom. May I accept you as my Savior instead of striving after my own goodness. And may you remind me of your grace whenever I forget the gospel. I pray in Jesus's name. Amen.

CHAPTER 6

SIN AS LEPROSY (PART 1)

2 Kings 5:1–19

¹ Now Naaman was commander of the army of the
king of Aram. He was a great man in the sight of his
master and highly regarded, because through him the
LORD had given victory to Aram. He was a valiant
soldier, but he had leprosy.

² Now bands from Aram had gone out and had
taken captive a young girl from Israel, and she served
Naaman's wife. ³ She said to her mistress, "If only my
master would see the prophet who is in Samaria! He
would cure him of his leprosy."

⁴ Naaman went to his master and told him what the girl from Israel had said. ⁵ "By all means, go," the king of Aram replied. "I will send a letter to the king of Israel." So Naaman left, taking with him ten talents of silver, six thousand shekels of gold and ten sets of clothing. ⁶ The letter that he took to the king of Israel read: "With this letter I am sending my servant Naaman to you so that you may cure him of his leprosy."

⁷ As soon as the king of Israel read the letter, he tore his robes and said, "Am I God? Can I kill and bring back to life? Why does this fellow send someone to me to be cured of his leprosy? See how he is trying to pick a quarrel with me!"

⁸ When Elisha the man of God heard that the king of Israel had torn his robes, he sent him this message: "Why have you torn your robes? Have the man come to me and he will know that there is a prophet in Israel." ⁹ So Naaman went with his horses and chariots and stopped at the door of Elisha's house. ¹⁰ Elisha sent a messenger to say to him, "Go, wash yourself seven times in the Jordan, and your flesh will be restored and you will be cleansed."

¹¹ But Naaman went away angry and said, "I thought that he would surely come out to me and stand and call on the name of the LORD his God, wave his hand over the spot and cure me of my

leprosy. [12] Are not Abana and Pharpar, the rivers of Damascus, better than any of the waters of Israel? Couldn't I wash in them and be cleansed?" So he turned and went off in a rage.

[13] Naaman's servants went to him and said, "My father, if the prophet had told you to do some great thing, would you not have done it? How much more, then, when he tells you, 'Wash and be cleansed'!"
[14] So he went down and dipped himself in the Jordan seven times, as the man of God had told him, and his flesh was restored and became clean like that of a young boy.

[15] Then Naaman and all his attendants went back to the man of God. He stood before him and said, "Now I know that there is no God in all the world except in Israel. Please accept now a gift from your servant."

[16] The prophet answered, "As surely as the LORD lives, whom I serve, I will not accept a thing." And even though Naaman urged him, he refused.

[17] "If you will not," said Naaman, "please let me, your servant, be given as much earth as a pair of mules can carry, for your servant will never again make burnt offerings and sacrifices to any other god but the LORD. [18] But may the LORD forgive your servant for this one thing: When my master enters the temple of Rimmon to bow down and he

is leaning on my arm and I bow there also—when I bow down in the temple of Rimmon, may the LORD forgive your servant for this."

[19] "Go in peace," Elisha said.

S econd Kings 5 tells the story of Naaman the Syrian, and every part of the story is important. This account is one of the most wonderful illustrations in all of the Bible about the nature of and the cure for sin. Naaman had everything: He was a great man, highly regarded, highly decorated, and very wealthy. But he had leprosy, a sickness that the Bible often uses as a metaphor for sin. Actual leprosy (many unrelated skin conditions were also called leprosy at the time) disfigured the body, progressed relentlessly, and had no cure. It was a fatal and isolating sickness. And Naaman had it. In most ways, he had a seemingly perfect life, and yet something was eating away at him.

The ancient Greeks had a sense of the tragic nature of life. In fact, they invented the art form known as "tragedy"— stories about a great man or woman who was accomplished and respected but had a fatal flaw. That flaw could be pride or jealousy or the inability to control oneself or the failure to be courageous or a denial of the truth. But Oedipus and Antigone aren't the only ones with flaws. Behind these stories is the profound insight that no matter how great our life may seem or how impressive we are, we all have something wrong with us.

The story of Naaman reveals what the flaw is: leprosy of the heart. No matter how good things may seem, sin makes each of our lives a tragedy—unless God intervenes. That is what happened for Naaman: God showed him the leprosy in his heart and how to be healed of it.

We can categorize this passage's teachings under three headings. The story tells us what Naaman really needed to be cured of; what the nature of his cure was; and, finally, how we know he *was* cured.

What Really Needed Curing

The text shows us that Naaman's problem is not primarily his leprosy. Many times when a sick person approaches Jesus in the Gospels, he deals with them on two levels. Take, for example, when the paralytic is lowered through a roof by his friends so that he can get to Jesus and be healed. Jesus says, "Son, your sins are forgiven" (Mark 2:5).

That's not what the paralyzed man and his friends went to all that trouble for. They wanted him to be able to walk. But that isn't what Jesus immediately addresses. It's not that Jesus isn't concerned about the man's ailment. Jesus *is* moved by physical suffering, and in this case he does something to fix it. But first he talks about the man's sins. He wants the man to understand something: *My son, I'm going to heal your body, but do you know what your biggest problem is? Do you know what's really killing you? It's the sin in your heart.*

We have to be careful here, because in several other places in the Bible Jesus makes clear that the reason one person is sicker than another is not because the first person is more sinful. Several times in the Gospels, people ask Jesus whether someone is blind or suffering because they are more sinful than others, and Jesus says no. In Luke 13, for example, he refers to eighteen people who died in a tower collapse and rejects the idea that they were somehow more sinful. But then he immediately says, "But unless you repent, you too will all perish" (v. 5). What Jesus is saying is that, in general, the brokenness of this world is due to its real, underlying problem: sin. The visible problems are the result of an invisible problem. And when the brokenness in your life opens your eyes to the deeper brokenness in your heart, it can become the very way God leads you to his grace and redemption.

God is dealing with Naaman here in this exact way. As you read the passage, one thing to note is that God could have cured Naaman the minute he walked in the door. Elisha could have waved his hand and cured him just the way Naaman expected. Yet time and again, Naaman is met with rebuffs, refusals, and humblings. The man shows up with 750 pounds of silver and 150 pounds of gold, and Elisha won't even come to the door to meet him personally. After Elisha sends a messenger to talk to him, Naaman goes away in a rage.

Why the runaround? Because God is after Naaman's pride. God is after his self-sufficiency. God is telling him, "Naaman, a leprosy of your heart is eating you up in a way that the leprosy of your body cannot. If you will let it, the outer leprosy can become the occasion for you to deal with the inner leprosy, the sin and pride that can kill you eternally."

Naaman's leprosy is pride, and the treatment he's prescribed is to be humbled again and again and again. But this problem isn't specific to just Naaman. Pride and self-sufficiency are growing in every one of our hearts, and it eats us up like leprosy too. It destroys our wisdom and our ability to love.

I once heard a mundane yet powerful illustration of this dynamic. A minister was asked to speak to two boarding schools in England, and after each message, he opened the floor for questions from the students.

The students at the first boarding school were flippant. None of them were all that interested in what the minister had to say. Rather than asking him real questions in pursuit of information or wisdom, they tried to trip him up by asking things they assumed he wouldn't know the answer to, like "Who did Cain marry?" They were clearly saying, "Look, we know what life is about. We don't need you to tell us anything."

Then the minister went to the second boarding school. The second boarding school was for students at least as bright as, if not brighter than, those at the first boarding school, but they all had cerebral palsy. "It was painful," he reflected. "If you know how this affects a person, the questions very often would take two minutes to get out." But he said there was an incredible difference between those two schools. "It's not that the kids in the second school (the kids with cerebral palsy) were more open to the gospel, that they were more believing, or anything like that. In fact, some of their questions were very pointed. 'Why did God let this happen to me?' was one of them. What was so different was that these kids had no conceit. None of that flippancy. They knew not only that the world was not their oyster, as the kids in the first school thought, but that it's not *anybody's* oyster. Life is hard. Existence and the problems of existence are profound. They wanted to get into what is meaning and what is destiny and why do we die?"

Do you know what the minister concluded?

The realization struck him as he said it: We are all born the same way as students at the first school. That posture is as natural as breathing. We grow up self-sufficient, thinking, "Don't tell me what to do. I know what I'm doing. I can handle life." But this attitude will destroy us unless something comes along and knocks it out of us.

The kids in the second boarding school had suffered, and therefore, they weren't as shallow as those in the first. They weren't superficial because they weren't proud. They saw they had reason to bow before the brokenness of life. Their outer brokenness caused them to consider these profound spiritual questions.

How does pride kill love and wisdom? Because we feel the need to carefully protect the little self-image that says, "I can handle life." In the first twenty years of life, at least (probably even the first forty years of life, from what I can tell), the information that says, "No, you can't handle life," is screened out. The only information we allow in is whatever builds up the self-image. As a result, our wisdom is compromised. Our love is drained, because proud people can love others only to the degree that it benefits themselves. We tune out the truth until we end up doing something so foolish that we're forced to admit we don't know what we're doing.

This is an inner leprosy in us all, and it has to be cured. The question is how.

The Nature of the Cure

As we've already seen, God deals with Naaman by insulting him at every turn: flattening his pride and going after the roots of his self-esteem and demolishing them. I know this sounds pretty strange, but this is how God's cure always starts. The gospel comes to us just the way it came to Naaman. In the beginning, it's nothing but an insult. It always starts that way.

In the beginning, the gospel levels our self-image. Eventually, it gives us a self-view much greater than anything we could ever conceive of on our own. But not at first. And notice how I used the term *self-view*, not *self-image*. A self-image is almost always something we concoct within ourselves. But the gospel, if we let it do its dirty work, will give us a view of ourselves (a wonder and a glory of a reality about who we are) beyond anything we could ever aspire to without it.

Before you can build a palace, however, you have to clear the site of the debris already there. This can be a painful process. The demands of the gospel—and its tearing down our own pridefulness—are insulting. The outside of the gospel is bitter at first bite, but the inside is infinitely sweet.

Three principles of the gospel's cure were extremely hard for a pagan man like Naaman to swallow. Each one challenged his old, proud way of thinking about himself and about life. And even though he was a pagan over two thousand years ago and we're modern people of today, there is a tremendous amount of commonality between the convictions of both eras.

First, the simplicity of the cure offends Naaman. In verse 10, Elisha's messenger tells him simply to "wash yourself seven times in the Jordan, and your flesh will be restored and you will be cleansed." Pagans loved—and expected—religious salvation to be elaborate, dramatic, and impressive. All the pagan religions in those days (or even now) involved features like these, such as mysterious figures in beautiful garments going through complicated rituals and speaking mysterious incantations.

If you want a great example of how pagans understood religion, look at Mozart's opera *The Magic Flute*. It's based on Egyptian mystery religions, and at its climax, two of the main characters, Tamino and Pamina, must pass through four dimensions to find salvation. They pass through air, earth, fire, and water as they overcome ordeals and progressively work their way toward liberation. As the title suggests, they have a magic flute to aid them, as well as the power of their love and the courage of their hearts and a set of elaborate instructions given to them by priests.

This is the sort of journey Naaman is expecting. He envisions Elisha, one of the most important men in Israel, making a grand show of meeting him, waving his hands over him, and pronouncing him miraculously healed. Instead, Elisha sends a servant to tell Naaman to take a bath. "This is too simple," Naaman thinks. "Just wash, repent, believe? Come on. There has to be more to it than that." But, no, there isn't anything more to it than that.

We modern people are a lot like pagans. Why do you think New Age mentality and many cultic groups are still flourishing? Because their approach is mystical, entailing processes that are often complex. These processes involve an intoxicating blend of elaborate instructions, drama, and sensationalism, just like Tamino and Pamina moving up through the realms.

In contrast, Elisha says, "Go, wash." I can't tell you how many times I have explained the basic message of the gospel and heard people reply, "It's too easy." They're insulted by how simple it is, just as Naaman was.

Second, the freeness of the cure offends Naaman. If you pay close attention to the passage, you can see that Naaman's servants understand this as the real source of his frustration. As Naaman leaves Elisha's house, the servants come up and say, "If the prophet had told you to do some great thing, would you not have done it?" (v. 13). In other words, if Elisha had asked Naaman to perform some great feat like rescuing captives or slaying a monster, he wouldn't have been insulted.

They see what Naaman doesn't: that Naaman wants to make God a partner in his salvation. He wants to do God a favor so God will do him a favor. Naaman doesn't want charity; he wants an equivalent exchange. He doesn't want a relationship; he wants a business transaction. Notice how he even brings a royal letter so he can impress God and Elisha by boasting about all the important people he knows.

In addition, he brings an enormous treasure. He thinks God and his prophet will *have* to cure him when he shows them how he can enrich them for doing so. He wants to show them that he can make God's temple the wealthiest place in all the land. Not only that, but he is also a man of incredible agility, remarkable strength, and military genius. He's a man of prowess, and he's ready to do anything.

This is why the freeness and simplicity of God's instructions are insulting. He knows that in all the legends and tales of glory, everybody gets excited when the hero says, "What must I do to be saved?" They are always told to do some great deed or slay some dragon. Take Hercules, for example, who was given twelve impossible labors to perform.

If Elisha had said to Naaman, "Bring me the broomstick of the Wicked Witch of the West," Naaman would have replied, "Now you're talking." Instead, he's left thinking, "Take a bath? Any idiot can do that." Naaman is offended that any person, even without money, prowess, goodness, morality, or anything else, has free access to such salvation. What he's really asking is, "Are you saying nothing about me matters a bit? Nothing about me can merit, earn, or attract the cure of God? Everything is worthless?" Elisha's response is essentially, "Yeah. Everything."

The reason Naaman goes off in a rage is that in this exchange he perceives the principle that Paul articulates many centuries later in Romans 3:22–23: "There is no difference, for all have sinned and fall short of the glory of God."

Paul is pointing out that when it comes to the cure of God, there is no difference between the most upstanding citizen and the most hardened criminal. The pagan, as well as the modern person, replies, "How could anybody ever say that?" The answer is found in considering the leprosy of pride in each of our hearts, no matter who we are.

Religious people experience a pride that causes them to think, "I'm better than most people because of my spiritual accomplishments. God owes me, life owes me, and other people owe me." They try to make God a partner in their salvation just as Naaman did. Their attitude toward God is, *You do me favors because I've done you favors.* By contrast, the irreligious experience a pride that causes them to think, "I'm not going to let God tell me what to do. Nobody tells me how to live my life. I choose what I'm going to do. I am my own religion. I am my own morality."

No difference exists between these two attitudes. Both kinds of people are their own lord and their own savior. Both are inflicted with spiritual leprosy, and their wisdom and love are eaten up by it. It doesn't matter who you are, who you know, what you've done, or how rich you are. There is no difference.

The third aspect of the cure that offends Naaman is its exclusivity. Note what he says: "Are not Abana and Pharpar, the rivers of Damascus, better than any of the waters of Israel? Couldn't I wash in them and be cleansed?" (2 Kings 5:12). To Naaman, restricting the cure to one river is silly and narrow-minded. If that's the way it is to be done and there really is no difference in who gets cured, why not anywhere?

Why not in his own rivers? Here, the pagan mind is just like the modern mind. Modern people are just as offended by the New Testament's message as pagans were offended by the Old Testament's message. The pagans felt that because every people had their own god, there were many paths to salvation. Modern people are just as offended by this idea. Why is going to God through Jesus the *only* way to be saved? Why does it have to be *this* river?

But the gospel is simple and free *because* it's exclusive; if it weren't, it wouldn't be either of those things. These attributes all go together because if they didn't, the claim of the gospel would fall apart. How does exclusivity make salvation accessible to us all? Take, for example, a common response to the biblical story today: "I don't believe you have to be a Christian to be saved. I believe any good person can find salvation—anyone who is disciplined, does what's right, or seeks goodness and truth. Anyone who's really seeking to be saved will be saved."

Do you see what's going on? That salvation isn't simple anymore, and it's certainly not free. The only way you can say, "There are many paths to God," is by saying, "Good works are really what will get you to the top." You have to deny the concept of grace itself. And these beliefs also contain a hidden exclusiveness in them. They attempt to make salvation inclusive, and yet they reject anyone who doesn't fit the speaker's standard of morality, goodness, and truth.

If any "good person" can make it to heaven, what about

the morally disabled? What about the person who has made a mess of their life and is now on their deathbed? What about the misbehaving child? Even this seemingly tolerant world-view has a bias toward the strong and the good over the weak and the bad. By contrast, the gospel says that anybody can come—good and bad, strong and weak—as long as they're humble. The exclusivity of Christianity is the requirement of humility.

We all know deep down that to fix what is wrong with us, something great must be done. Naaman understood it. We all understand it today. But many of us try to do the great thing ourselves. We believe we will become whole if we are kind or accepting of others, if we get the right job, if we become rich, if we realize our sexual desires, if we spread enough love in the world, or if we champion the right political causes. A Christian is somebody willing to say, "I could never do what is required to save myself. But someone has done a great thing *for* me. Somebody has passed through the earth, fire, water, and air so that I may be saved."

In Exodus 15, God's people came to poisoned water and a tree was cut down and thrown into the water to make it drinkable. God said, "I am the LORD, who heals you" (v. 26). In the same way, Jesus was cut down and thrown into the justice of God to do the great thing we cannot do. As Jesus himself said to his disciples, "Can you drink the cup I drink or be baptized with the baptism I am baptized with?" (Mark 10:38).

Isaiah 53:5 says that "by his wounds we are healed." Our leprosy was put on Jesus. As he fell apart, we came together.

The Certainty of Naaman's Cure

Naaman finally did follow the instructions he was given. He went down to the water. Can you imagine how he must have felt? I'm sure he didn't say right away, "Ah, I get it." He likely thought, "I don't quite understand this, and maybe I'm crazy, but I'm going to try it." And something changed. The gospel got through. All the insults he had suffered began to humble him. And when he came up again, his skin was like that of a young boy, pure and spotless. What a picture of the gospel!

No matter what you've done, no matter how warped or afflicted you are, when you *receive* God's salvation instead of trying to *achieve* it, the minute you believe, in God's sight you are instantly as pure and spotless and unsullied as if you'd never sinned. Naaman's skin became spotless, but that's not all—something happened inside Naaman too. The spiritual leprosy was healed, or at least it was being healed. How do we know?

Four signs show that his pride had been dealt with. First, his thinking had changed. The Christian experience is more than a way of thinking, but it is not less. It is a mystical experience, but it is not just a mystical experience. Naaman's worldview changed. His reasoning was awakened. Certain ideas became compelling to him. He went back to Elisha and admitted that even though he is a polytheist, now he knows "there is no God in all the world except in Israel" (2 Kings 5:15).

A Christian does not simply say, "Well, my views haven't changed, but I've sensed a sort of presence in my life." The gospel is more than a vague, mystical experience. There are certain truths about God and about yourself that you must understand as the realities that they are. Our minds must be awakened just as Naaman's was.

Second, Naaman became radically generous. Immediately after he was healed, he tried to offer Elisha a gift of his own free will. When you're proud, you have to continually accrue. You have to take more and more to keep building your self-image. But following Christ changes the whole flow of your life from "You give to me" to "I give to you." The things we thought of as our own no longer seem like our property but rather as opportunities to bless others. A radical generosity of not only money but also time, energy, and everything else is a sign of real conversion.

Third, Naaman became a servant. He explicitly labeled himself as such to Elisha. In the next chapter, we'll take a deeper look at this change of heart and its ramifications, but allow me to make a brief point about it here: Naaman was saying that God is his master (v. 17).

If you follow God to do him favors so he will do you favors, you're not treating him as a master; you're treating him as a partner. You believe he owes you and you owe him.

Therefore, you believe there are limits to what he can ask of you.

If God has given us everything sheerly of his own grace—if everything we have ever done or accomplished accounts for nothing—there are no limits or conditions on our obedience to him. He can ask us anything. He's not our partner; he's our Master.

I hate to insult the cat lovers reading this, but let me tell you something about the difference between cats and dogs. Dogs have masters. In all the movies about dogs, when the master gets into trouble and tells their dog, "Go get help, girl!" the dog always gets help.

I have a cat we love very much, but I know this: If I broke my leg in front of the cat and told it, "Go get help, girl!" the cat would look at me and say, "*Me?*" Dogs have masters; cats have housekeepers. They need you, but they definitely don't serve you.

Is God your master, or is he your housekeeper? You may be convinced you need him, but that isn't sufficient: A cat knows it can't live without us. The question is, Are you placing limitations on what God can ask of you? If so, you aren't a servant. The sign of conversion is that all the limits are gratefully gone. As Isaac Watts's 1707 hymn "When I Survey the Wondrous Cross" goes,

> Were the whole realm of nature mine,
> That were a present far too small;

Love so amazing, so divine,
Demands my soul, my life, my all.

Amazingly, Naaman asked Elisha for a quantity of Israel's dirt to take back to his homeland. He knew he would have to return to serve his king by accompanying him to the temple of Rimmon and bowing down, but he asked Elisha for a concession.

Naaman would bow to perform his duty to his country and his people, but right beside him would be a servant with earth from Israel. That servant would put the earth on the ground, and Naaman would let everyone know that when he knelt down, he wasn't praying to Rimmon. He would never sacrifice to any other god but the God of Israel.

Fourth, Naaman realized there is no difference among those to whom grace is given. This final mark of his conversion is an extremely important one. Notice how he didn't say to Elisha, "I don't want to go back to those awful pagans. They might contaminate me. They don't understand God like you and I do."

A lot of people who profess to be Christians feel that way. Their attitude is, *I don't want to be out in the world. I don't want to be out in the professions, out in the market, out in the schools. I only want to be around Christians who believe like me. I don't want to be contaminated.* I wonder whether people who think this way have ever been cured of their pride as Naaman was.

Naaman realized that God had now prepared him to love

his people and serve his king better than ever before, all while he let them know whom he was really doing it for. He would not only serve but also find a way to be a witness to the one true God.

Christians today must respond to God's grace with this same vision. After we are saved, we can't simply withdraw from the world and keep the good news to ourselves. If we do, it is proof that we don't understand the gospel at all. If we are so private and cowardly as to not let the people around us know why we believe what we believe and why we're living the way we're living, we aren't really following God at all. We aren't truly grateful to him.

Without obnoxiousness and pride and condescension, but also without cowardice, Naaman decides he will live his life in front of everyone in Aram, letting them know who the real God is. There is no compromise in his attitude: *I'm going to try to love my country while honoring my God, but if they won't have me, so be it. I will never, ever sacrifice to any other god but the God of Israel.*

To this day, there are plenty of places with plenty of people who won't allow you to even whisper that you're a Christian, no matter how kind or humble or loving you are. They may silence you, ostracize you, or even persecute you. Even so, we must not forget these marks of a converted person. Our minds must stay awakened. We must become radically generous. We must become servants. And we must gladly and fully submit all we have and all we are to God's will, living every dimension of our lives—public and private—in alignment with who he is.

Some reading this may still think they're not as bad as the gospel says. They may believe it primitive to think we're all sinners and only the death of the Son of God can save us. They believe they'll do life fine on their own. Let me remind you that Naaman had the best life anyone could have hoped for—and yet he still had leprosy, not just in his flesh but also in his heart. The spiritual leprosy of your heart will ruin your life just the way his leprosy ruined his.

If you believe that, or if you've already seen it happen, I'm here to tell you it doesn't matter how deeply stained you are. It doesn't matter what you've done. There's a cure that is simple and free. Repent and believe.

And if any of you are unwilling to live your faith publicly, remember Naaman's example. Just as Naaman insisted on bringing the soil of Israel to the outside world, we are to bring the gospel of grace everywhere. It was symbolic for Naaman, but it is actual for us.

Did you know that Jesus Christ himself preached about Naaman? And when the audience understood the sermon, they tried to kill him. In Luke 4:27, when Jesus was speaking in the synagogue of his hometown of Nazareth, he concluded his sermon by saying, "There were many in Israel with leprosy in the time of Elisha the prophet, yet not one of them was cleansed—only Naaman the Syrian." Because of that statement, everyone in the synagogue tried to throw him off a cliff. Why? He was telling them, "The one true God doesn't belong just to you. He's the God of *everyone.*"

If we believe in grace and follow Jesus, our pride will be dissolved and the leprosy of our hearts will be cured. We will feel concern for others, give to them, and serve them so that they may know the wonderful truth we've discovered through the gospel. We will point them to the very salvation we have received ourselves.

A PRAYER FOR HUMILITY

Thank you, Father, for giving me the time to consider the cure for my pride and self-sufficiency. I pray that you will apply your grace to my heart in the diverse ways in which this great passage can be applied. Show me the lack of marks of conversion in my life and in my attitude toward you. Convict me of my sin and need for you. Strengthen my servanthood. Help me make you my Master. Turn my heart toward those in the world who don't know you, and help me show them your grace. As you apply these truths to me, help me continue to treasure and ponder them in my heart through your Holy Spirit. In Jesus's name I pray. Amen.

CHAPTER 7

SIN AS LEPROSY (PART 2)

2 Kings 5:1–3, 19–27

¹ Now Naaman was commander of the army of the king of Aram. He was a great man in the sight of his master and highly regarded, because through him the LORD had given victory to Aram. He was a valiant soldier, but he had leprosy.

² Now bands from Aram had gone out and had taken captive a young girl from Israel, and she served Naaman's wife. ³ She said to her mistress, "If only my master would see the prophet who is in Samaria! He would cure him of his leprosy." . . .

¹⁹ After Naaman had traveled some distance, ²⁰ Gehazi, the servant of Elisha the man of God, said to himself, "My master was too easy on Naaman, this Aramean, by not accepting from him what he brought. As surely as the LORD lives, I will run after him and get something from him."

²¹ So Gehazi hurried after Naaman. When Naaman saw him running toward him, he got down from the chariot to meet him. "Is everything all right?" he asked.

²² "Everything is all right," Gehazi answered. "My master sent me to say, 'Two young men from the company of the prophets have just come to me from the hill country of Ephraim. Please give them a talent of silver and two sets of clothing.'"

²³ "By all means, take two talents," said Naaman. He urged Gehazi to accept them, and then tied up the two talents of silver in two bags, with two sets of clothing. He gave them to two of his servants, and they carried them ahead of Gehazi. ²⁴ When Gehazi came to the hill, he took the things from the servants and put them away in the house. He sent the men away and they left. ²⁵ Then he went in and stood before his master Elisha.

"Where have you been, Gehazi?" Elisha asked.

"Your servant didn't go anywhere," Gehazi answered. ²⁶ But Elisha said to him, "Was not my spirit with you when the man got down from his chariot to meet you? Is this the time to take money, or to accept clothes, olive groves, vineyards, flocks, herds, or menservants and maidservants? [27] Naaman's leprosy will cling to you and to your descendants forever." Then Gehazi went from Elisha's presence and he was leprous, as white as snow.

In the previous chapter, we learned how the first part of Naaman's story reveals something essential about the nature of sin and its cure. In this chapter, we'll examine the second part of Naaman's story, which reveals another facet of the nature of sin and how God addresses it. What we will see is that Naaman continually goes to kings to better his life, yet God insists on speaking to him through servants. Naaman repeatedly seeks the company of somebodies, but God introduces him to salvation through nobodies. And that is a crucial lesson for us today.

Notice that Naaman first gets the idea to visit Elisha from a captured slave girl. And remember that later he is given instructions for the cure from the servant of Elisha. And remember, too, that Naaman's own servants understand the message of the gospel before Naaman does. They are the ones who calm his rage and explain it to him.

What does this tell us about ourselves and about God? We can draw at least four important principles from this account:

- The world cannot solve our deepest problems.
- We must see that there is a prophet in Israel.
- God speaks through the humble, the marginal, and the uncool.
- We need to emulate the little slave girl.

Let's look at them.

The World Cannot Solve Our Deepest Problems

Despite being told by his wife's servant to go to the prophet Elisha, Naaman decides to go to the king of Israel and ask him for a cure. His assumption about the nature of religion is exactly the same as the assumptions of the educated classes of our society today. Here's how that works.

Throughout history, if you wanted to receive a miracle from the god of a specific country, you first had to go to its king. Why? Because religion was basically a form of social control. The king was usually seen either as a mediator of the gods or as a god himself. The king bankrolled the priests and the prophets and the magicians, and their job was to support the power structure just as the king supported them. If somebody in Egypt had a dream they wanted interpreted, for example, they would first go to the pharaoh, and the pharaoh would summon his court of holy men to try to divine its meaning.

In the late 1800s, the educated classes of Europe and America rejected the idea of a supernatural God. They returned to the view that Naaman had—that religion is basically an expression of culture and an extension of human power. *Religion is just a way for a culture to get a kind of cohesion. Every culture has its own god. That's fine! It's just a way for cultures to give answers to their own questions. It provides a sort of social glue.*

One of the implications of this view is that as human beings we are ultimately on our own. If we want to deal with poverty, oppression, and psychological distress, we must find human-created solutions. We have to go to the king. We have to ask the government. We have to ask big businesses. We have to ask psychologists or sociologists. We have to create a blue-ribbon committee to solve our issues. We have to go to the top people, you see, because that's all we have.

This is not how it works with the gospel. Naaman doesn't realize he has gone to the only country in the world where the prophets are not puppets of the king. The king of Israel tells him what the politicians, sociologists, and psychologists of our day ought to tell us: "Am I God?" (2 Kings 5:7). In other words, the king tells Naaman, "Do not come to me for what only God can do. Don't you realize your deepest problems can't be solved by human means?"

A perfect illustration of this truth is a story told by Rebecca Pippert, a Christian writer who took a class at Harvard in counseling and psychology. One day she heard the professor sharing a case study in which a particular man's hatred for his mother had destroyed his life. She recalls,

> One of the courses I audited at Harvard was called "Systems of Counseling." We were looking at a case study in which the therapist . . . helped the patient uncover a hidden hostility toward his mother.
>
> . . . Then the professor began to proceed to the next case. Mustering my courage, I raised my hand and said, ". . . Let's say the patient returned a few weeks later and said, 'I'm so relieved to understand what was bothering me. My mother did things that provoked my hostility. But now I'd like to get beyond my anger. I'd like to be able to love her and forgive her. How do I do that?' How does psychodynamic psychotherapy help a person with a request like this?"
>
> There was silence. Then the professor answered, "I think the therapist would say, 'Lots of luck!' . . . To ask that his hostility magically disappear isn't realistic. He'll have to learn to live with it and hopefully not be driven by

it. . . . If you guys are looking for a changed heart, I think you're looking in the wrong department."[1]

What he said stunned the students. The professor was echoing the king of Israel: "Am I God?" He was saying that science can never give anyone a forgiving heart. Science can tell you what *is*, but it can never tell you what *ought to be*.

As soon as you set foot in the territory of guilt and forgiveness and of discerning what's right and what's wrong, you've left the realm of technical expertise. You've entered the realm of faith and spirituality.

This is not to say that politics and sociology and psychology aren't important. But our deepest problems in life—the ones that have us asking, "Who am I? What is the meaning of life? What is right and wrong?"—are things that human endeavor and expertise cannot solve at all. To answer these questions, we must go to God.

See That There Is a Prophet in Israel

Verse 8 reads, "When Elisha the man of God heard that the king of Israel had torn his robes, he sent him this message: 'Why have you torn your robes? Have the man come to me and he will know that there is a prophet in Israel.'" Elisha knows Naaman will be cured only if he sees there is a prophet in Israel, not just a king.

One of the great conceits of the modern world is that we think we're searching for God, but the reality is that we aren't. Most books or documentaries on world religions say humanity has been searching for God for centuries, but the apostle Paul comes right out in Romans 3:11, quoting Psalm 14:2–3, and rejects that notion: "There is no one . . . who seeks God." C. S. Lewis observes that the idea that human beings are searching for God is as absurd as saying the mice are searching for the cat.[2] We are not searching for God. What we're searching for is satisfaction. We're searching for a god we can concoct—one who is comfortable—rather than the real God.

We see this with Naaman's approach. He came with money. He was looking for a god who could be bought. He expected a god with limited authority, whose salvation he could earn. But Naaman soon realized that this is not a tame god but a wild God—and that this wild God is met through the prophets and apostles through whom he reveals himself.

This is why we will never truly find the real God until we read the Bible. Why? Because the authors of the books of the Bible are the prophets and apostles through whom God reveals himself. You may read that and think, "How closed-minded! I think people can find and put together their own faith without having to read Scripture."

But that attitude will prevent you from finding the radical religion that can change your life. We could never piece together an image of God that depicts his full, true self. If we put together a faith without the testimony of the prophets and apostles, we will inevitably conjure up a god who acts the way we want. He does everything we like and nothing we don't. This is a god who will never surprise or amaze us. This is not a wild god; this is a housebroken god.

We will see the real God for who he is only if we're willing to tell ourselves, "There is a God who has revealed himself through the biblical accounts of his prophets and apostles, and I will submit myself to what he says about himself. I will not search him out; I will be searched out by him." This is the only way to have a radical religion that stands a chance at helping us.

If we don't know there is a prophet in Israel, we have a god of our own making, and our leprosy will persist.

God Speaks Through the Humble, the Marginal, and the Uncool

Consider the slave girl who told Naaman about Elisha. This was a Hebrew girl whose family had been destroyed. The Syrian band of soldiers probably came up over the Golan Heights and marauded and pillaged the Israelites, killing some people and bringing back others as slaves.

This girl was at the bottom of the social ladder. She was a female. She was a child, probably between the ages of ten and twelve years old. She was a foreigner taken out of her homeland. And, of course, she was a slave. In the eyes of the Syrians, she was barely one step above livestock. And God spoke through her.

In general, it is the humble, the uncool, the uneducated, the poor, and the unsuccessful—the people on the margins—who grasp the gospel most quickly. Why, as we saw in the last chapter, did Naaman's servants understand the gospel before he did? Because those at the bottom of the social ladder know how hard life is. They know how weak people are. They know firsthand the reality of human sin. By contrast, people who have success, wealth, or power often stay deluded about these things. When the gospel (that we're all sinners who need to be saved by grace alone, not anything we can do) is shared, it is the people who have experienced failure, oppression, marginalization, and hardship who are usually the first to understand.

From this, we can draw a point that is both theological and practical. Theologically, it reflects how God often communicates. For example, in the book of Genesis, God's answer to Pharaoh's troubled dreams comes through Joseph, a slave in a dungeon. In 1 Samuel, when the Israelites are at war with the Philistines, none of the great warriors stand a chance against the mighty Goliath—except little David and his slingshot. And out of all the great countries of the day—Assyria, Babylon, Greece, and Rome—God chooses to go to a small nation of Jews and says, "I'm going to reveal myself to the world through you."

The ultimate example of this principle, however, is Jesus. Jesus wasn't born in Rome or Athens—or even Jerusalem. He was born in a manger and raised in the small village of Nazareth. He was raised poor. He gave his kingdom to illiterate fishermen. He died a criminal's death.

Throughout Jesus's entire ministry, the kings, philosophers, and great people of the world knew nothing about him. Nothing! When his disciples first started to preach the gospel, how did the great people respond? They laughed. They said what the great people today still say: that the solution to the world's problems will come from the throne rooms and drawing rooms, the lecture halls and political floors, the convention centers and the studios in Hollywood, not from the slave quarters and fishing boats.

But the solution did come from those lowly places, and here's why: If Jesus had come as a somebody, he never would have been crucified. Somebodies don't get crucified. Nobodies do. Jesus had to be a nobody so that he could die on the cross and God could both pay for our sins and save us at the same time—so he could be both just and justifier. That is the wisdom and power of God.

The weakness and defeat on the cross became the great triumph. The somebody became nobody so that we nobodies could become somebodies. That's the gospel.

Here's the practical application of God revealing himself through these types of people. During my time as a pastor in New York City, I noticed something. Many of the people

I preached to lived in Manhattan—the most developed and influential of the city's boroughs. These people were smart and generally well-off. Many of them were at the top of their fields. But most of the Christians in New York didn't—and still don't—live in Manhattan. They live on the fringes of the city, in the Bronx and in Queens. There, things are less slick. The buildings aren't as tall. The people are not as self-consciously sophisticated. And they often understand sin and grace before those in Manhattan with high profiles and fashionable lifestyles do.

If we see the gospel as credible only when it comes from the mouths of the famous, the attractive, and the accomplished, we will never mature in the gospel.

We may go to the kings, but God will continually speak to us through the servants.

Emulate the Little Slave Girl

Lastly, I want to urge the Christians reading this book to emulate the little slave girl. Against all odds, she reached Naaman. The chances of one of the great leaders of the ancient world finding the God of Israel were infinitesimal, but God used this girl to reach Namaan and to shake the counsels of the mighty.

Do you know why she was able to do it? She paid the price of usefulness. What do I mean by that phrase? I'll explain. First, though, notice that she contrasts with another servant—Gehazi, who served Elisha. Unlike Gehazi, the little girl was in a dismal position: She was almost certainly an orphan after an invading army killed her parents and kidnapped her. As a result, she could look forward only to a life of utter servitude, total loneliness, and complete ruin. On the other hand, Gehazi was serving under the prophet of Israel, which meant he was next in line for the position. You would think that if somebody was going to do something useful for God, it would be Gehazi. Yet it is the little girl who changed history and Gehazi who is remembered as an utter failure, stricken with leprosy. Why? It's because in the silence of each of their hearts, she paid the price of usefulness, and he did not.[3]

The contrast between the little girl and Gehazi is highlighted when Elisha refuses Naaman's generous gift after his healing, despite no prohibition against prophets accepting gifts. When Elisha refuses to take Naaman's money, it's not because there is any prohibition on giving to prophets and priests. After all, believers were required to tithe in the Old Testament. But Elisha knows it is not the right moment for doing so. "Is this the time to take money?" he asks Gehazi.

It is not the right time because Naaman is a new convert who is used to pagan religions. In those contexts, you paid to be saved and you earned salvation, and every holy man likely had his hand held out. Elisha is discipling Naaman from the beginning, helping him see that God does not need anything from him, that the gospel is different from any other religion, and that the true God is different from any other god.

So Elisha refuses to take money even though Naaman could have made him incredibly rich. The minute Naaman leaves, however, Gehazi goes running after him. He lies to Naaman to get money for himself, and he even asks for a little less than he wants because he knows he'll get more by doing so. He asks for one talent, and he gets two. How could someone who has been training for years to be a man of God do this?

The reason can only be that for years, deep in his heart, he had been dreaming of being like Naaman. He had fantasized about all the things the world could give him. By contrast, Elisha was done with craving what the world can give—this is seen in his rejecting Naaman's treasure—and as a result, God could use him.

Gehazi, however, had spent years dreaming of wealth and success. The minute he got near Naaman, therefore, he fell to temptation and was cursed with leprosy.

We may read of Gehazi's fate and think, "How cruel of God to curse him like that. Why would God do such a thing?" But consider the wisdom in God's judgment here. Gehazi's desire was to become Naaman—so he became Naaman. The most just punishment is for God to give someone exactly what they want. Unless we say to God, "Thy will be done," someday God will turn to us and say, "*Thy* will be done." And that is a terrible judgment. God gave Gehazi only what Gehazi wanted.

The slave girl had the same temptation. Think of all the nights she must have cried herself to sleep. Wouldn't she want justice? Wouldn't she want revenge? Wouldn't she want her father back? But in her heart, she must have said, "Lord, I want justice, but you're my Judge, and you're enough. I want a father, but you are my Father, and you're enough."

How do we know she did that? Look at what she says. Her words reveal that she has forgiven Naaman, the leader of the military operations that destroyed her family and took away her freedom. She forgave him to the point that when he is sick, she says, "If only my master would see the prophet who is in Samaria!" (2 Kings 5:3). There is love in her words: "If only!"

She doesn't say, "Ha! He has leprosy, the old goat. Another finger fell off today. Good! May he rot in hell." She no longer needed or dreamed about the things the world could give. She didn't want the justice of the world. She thought, "God is my Judge." She no longer sought a father of the world. Instead, she thought, "Lord, if you're the only Father I get, you're enough."

She let her suffering make her want worldly things less, not more. That is a lesson for us. When we suffer, either we can turn to God or we can let our hardship grow our desire for consolation in this world. She chose the first, and therefore, her heart became great. Don't you think the reason Naaman listened to her in the first place was because he could see she loved him and his wife?

A lot of us are crying and wondering why God let terrible things happen to us. Perhaps he does it to make our hearts long for him. Our suffering can give us the chance to pay the price of usefulness. We can let our troubles move us closer to the world, bound to and desirous of it, or we can let our troubles create a great heart in us. We can be deeper in bondage, or we can be free.

Often we insist on thinking, "If only I knew why God let all these things happen." But we must remember that the little girl had no idea why she had been sent to Aram after her family was destroyed. She couldn't possibly have figured that out and thought, "Oh, I get it! If I let my suffering make my heart great, not only will my master be saved, but for the next three thousand years, people will read my story and be inspired by it."

Of course not. She didn't see the full picture, and we don't either. So if we think, "I could obey God if only I knew the reasons for my suffering," we aren't acting in true service. We are acting out of calculation. "Will I get the outcome I desire?" is always lurking in our minds.

But that is not the question the slave girl asked, and it is not what made her great. But it is what made Gehazi leprous. Pay the price of usefulness and you can become a light in a dark place and possibly shake the counsels of the great. God can use you in incredible ways because God uses nobodies.

Even more, be like the One who became leprous voluntarily, who lost his father voluntarily, who became a slave voluntarily, and was taken away from beauty and comfort and privilege and thrown into poverty and torment voluntarily. Be like the One who said, "Not my will, but yours be done" (Luke 22:42)—the true servant of all.

If Jesus Christ was able to do that for you in such a great way, look to him and you'll be able to do for him in your own small ways what the servant girl did for Naaman.

Once we become a Naaman by swallowing our pride, submitting to God, and receiving his grace, we have to become a servant. We have to go out and serve. When we work among the poor and the marginalized—especially if we are part of the cultural elite—we don't just go to them because they need us. We go because we need them as well.

We should expect to see wisdom in them. We should expect that when they hear the gospel—whether it's tomorrow or whether it was five years ago—we're going to learn from them. As much as we may keep going to kings, God goes to the nobodies. And thank him that he does, for such are we.

A PRAYER FOR HUMILITY

Father, thank you that there is a solution for my deepest problems. Help me remember that it's not like anything anybody expects. We don't go to the rulers. We don't go to the powerful. We go to the slave quarters. We go to nobodies. Father, help me understand the upside-down nature of the gospel. Turn me upside down, too, so that I find Jesus, who left his glory to become a servant. Lord, I want a God who works with little slave girls, not simply with kings. I thank you that you are a God like that, and I humble myself before you by your Spirit's help so that I can become as great as your Son was, who came not to be served but to serve and give his life as a ransom for many. It's in his name I pray this. Amen.

CHAPTER 8

SIN AS SLAVERY

Numbers 11:4–6, 10–20, 31–34

⁴ The rabble with them began to crave other food, and again the Israelites started wailing and said, "If only we had meat to eat! ⁵ We remember the fish we ate in Egypt at no cost—also the cucumbers, melons, leeks, onions and garlic. ⁶ But now we have lost our appetite; we never see anything but this manna!" . . .

¹⁰ Moses heard the people of every family wailing, each at the entrance to his tent. The LORD became exceedingly angry, and Moses was troubled. ¹¹ He asked the LORD, "Why have you brought this trouble

on your servant? What have I done to displease you that you put the burden of all these people on me? ¹² Did I conceive all these people? Did I give them birth? Why do you tell me to carry them in my arms, as a nurse carries an infant, to the land you promised on oath to their forefathers? ¹³ Where can I get meat for all these people? They keep wailing to me, 'Give us meat to eat!' ¹⁴ I cannot carry all these people by myself; the burden is too heavy for me. ¹⁵ If this is how you are going to treat me, put me to death right now—if I have found favor in your eyes—and do not let me face my own ruin."

¹⁶ The LORD said to Moses: "Bring me seventy of Israel's elders who are known to you as leaders and officials among the people. Have them come to the Tent of Meeting, that they may stand there with you. ¹⁷ I will come down and speak with you there, and I will take of the Spirit that is on you and put the Spirit on them. They will help you carry the burden of the people so that you will not have to carry it alone.

¹⁸ Tell the people: 'Consecrate yourselves in preparation for tomorrow, when you will eat meat. The LORD heard you when you wailed, "If only we had meat to eat! We were better off in Egypt!" Now the LORD will give you meat, and you will eat it. ¹⁹ You will not eat it for just one day, or two days, or five, ten or twenty days, ²⁰ but for a whole month—

until it comes out of your nostrils and you loathe it—
because you have rejected the LORD, who is among
you, and have wailed before him, saying, "Why did
we ever leave Egypt?"" . . .

³¹ Now a wind went out from the LORD and
drove quail in from the sea. It brought them down
all around the camp to about three feet above the
ground, as far as a day's walk in any direction. ³² All
that day and night and all the next day the people
went out and gathered quail. No one gathered less
than ten homers. Then they spread them out all
around the camp. ³³ But while the meat was still
between their teeth and before it could be consumed,
the anger of the LORD burned against the people, and
he struck them with a severe plague. ³⁴ Therefore the
place was named Kibroth Hattaavah, because there
they buried the people who had craved other food.

In the text we're examining in this chapter, from Numbers 11, the children of Israel are in the wilderness on their way to the promised land. Things aren't going well for them, to put it mildly. This is a dark passage; nobody lives happily ever after. What's more, unlike some of the other passages we've looked at, which have heroes like Naaman and his servants, here not a single person gives us a godly example.

But as dark as this story is, examining it is crucial because it tackles one of the most important questions about human nature: Why is it that even when we know the right thing to do, we still don't do it?

Slavery to Sin

In the last few pages of his book *The Abolition of Man*, C. S. Lewis compiles sayings from various world religions to highlight their near-universal agreement on which behaviors are encouraged and which are discouraged.[1]

For example, virtually all religions are against lying. They hold that we're not supposed to break our promises. We're not supposed to rob or murder each other. Instead, they all say we should respect each other. We're supposed to seek justice and equity. We're supposed to be generous with our possessions. In short, we're supposed to live by the Golden Rule—to treat everyone how we ourselves want to be treated.

All the religions that Lewis lists believe that this is the way we should live. And they also believe that the main reason for all the misery in the world is that we *don't* live this way.

So this raises the question: What is it about the human condition that makes it possible—perhaps even inevitable—that despite knowing exactly how we should live *and* knowing the consequences of not doing so, we nevertheless fail to live by that standard over and over again?

No matter who our therapist is, which philosophy we believe, whether our government is liberal or conservative or fascist or democratic, we all keep failing to do the right thing, to live the right way. We know what we should do. But we don't do it.

How can we explain that? The Bible's explanation is that human hearts are sinful. But more than that, the Bible tells us that we have become slaves to sin. The Bible says sin is not just an action; it's a power. Every sinful action has a destructive power on the faculty that chose that action. For example, when you sin with your mind, that sin shrivels your mind's rationality. When you sin with your heart, that sin shrivels your heart's emotions. When you sin with your will, that sin dissolves your willpower and self-control.

Sin is the suicidal action of the self harming the self. And no matter *how* we sin, doing so destroys our freedom and enslaves us. Look at the children of Israel in this passage, for example. After God has delivered them from slavery, what is their attitude? *We had a wonderful time in Egypt. Let's go back.*

Time and time again, the children of Israel crave the comforts of Egyptian civilization and want to go back even though doing so would mean returning to social, political, and economic slavery. Not only that, but returning to Egypt would result in them being treated worse than before, if not being flat-out annihilated. Anyone today reading this passage can easily think, "What idiots! How in the world can they want fish so bad that they'd let themselves become slaves again? Who would want to get whipped and beaten just for onions and garlic?" To any contemporary reader, the obvious thing to do is stick with the manna, however unappetizing it may be, and go on to the promised land. It's so clear what needs to be done, yet the Israelites can't do it. They won't do

it. They *don't* do it. Why not? Because they are still slaves—
not as they were in Egypt but slaves nonetheless: spiritual
slaves.

To be a political slave or an economic slave means you
have no power to do what's best for yourself. For example,
you might know the best thing for you is not to make bricks
but rather to be a dancer. But if you're a political or economic
slave, you are powerless to pursue the best use of your gifts
and talents. The children of Israel had been removed from
this type of slavery, but they remained subjected to a perni-
cious form of slavery. They were *spiritually* powerless to do
the right thing—unable to do what was best for them.

The Bible says every human being on the face of the earth
is a spiritual slave in this same way. Paul puts it like this in
Romans 7:18, 21: "For I have the desire to do what is good,
but I cannot carry it out. . . . So I find this law at work:
When I want to do good, evil is right there with me." He
summarizes the issue in verse 14: "We know that the law
is spiritual; but I am unspiritual, sold as a slave to sin." Paul
himself is telling us that the more he wants to do good, the
less he is able to do it. He is powerless to do what is good.
He is a slave.

Some people may read that and think, "That's an over-
statement, or at the very least it doesn't apply to me. I'm not
like Paul. I've never felt powerless to do what's right." But
look at what Paul is saying: The more he tries, the higher he
aspires to live, the more he is *aware* of his spiritual slavery,

which means if we aren't aware that we are spiritually enslaved, our moral ambition is too low.

For example, most everybody agrees with the Golden Rule. But if you think you have no problem living by that rule, I challenge you to try it for just twelve hours. For just one day, do unto others exactly as you would want to have people do to you. Half a day, in fact. Try to meet the needs of others with all the strength, joy, creativity, and speed with which you meet your own needs. Be as excited about their success as you would your own. If you try this, within a few hours—maybe within a few minutes—you'll find yourself thinking, "I see it now. The more I try to do good, the more I struggle to do it. The more I sense the powerlessness within me." And then you'll be able to say with Paul in verse 24, "What a wretched man I am! Who will rescue me from this body of death?"

We are spiritual slaves. We see what should be done, but we can't do it. And anybody who thinks they can simply hasn't tried very hard.

The Structure of Sin's Slavery

The second thing this story about the Israelites teaches us— and this is astonishing—is the structure of this slavery. As already noted, when we perform a sinful action, it isn't simply an action or a mistake that loses us points in heaven. It has a devastating effect on our freedom. Our capacity to want the good, to think the good, to understand the good, and even the will to *do* the good is undermined. As sin chips away at our minds, emotions, and resolve, we lose our freedom more and more.

We can see this in Numbers 11:4–6. First, verse 4 says the Israelites begin to "crave" the comforts of Egyptian civilization. I'll get back to that, but for now, see that this shows their emotions are being changed. Second, verse 5 says they remember that all the food they had in Egypt came with "no cost." This, as we saw earlier, is a form of denial: The cost of their eating in Egypt was their freedom. What's more, their craving is overwhelming their rationality. They are incapable of seeing that the cost of returning to Egypt would likely be death. Third, in verse 6 they say, "We have lost our appetite." The Hebrew there literally says, "Our soul is dried up." They have found themselves in a position where they don't want the manna anymore. Their very selves, their will to be, is dried up. Their memories of God's saving power in bringing them out of slavery has faded.

In the end, God gives them what they want. But the more they get of it, the less they love it. In the end, they have so much of what they want that it's coming out of their nostrils—and they loathe it.

This is the pattern of addiction. Not all addictions are sin, but the Bible shows us that all sin is addiction. Every sin, whether it's bitterness, envy, materialism, laziness, or sexual impurity, becomes an addiction.

Specific addictions, such as those to alcohol or drugs or pornography, are microcosms of how sin works in our lives more generally. Addiction starts like this: We feel some sort of disappointment or distress. As a result, we choose to deal with that distress using an agent, such as sex or alcohol. The agent promises transcendence, freedom, escape, or a sense of control, of being above whatever is discouraging us. But when we use these agents as a way of dealing with life, the trap is set. And as a result, three things happen.

First, our addiction, our sin, causes us to fall prey to what we might call the tolerance effect. This describes the way that the amount of alcohol or drugs—or the kind of sexual experience—we enjoy or need today will increase for us tomorrow. It won't be enough to fulfill us anymore. We need more than we had the day before. The more we give into the sin, the more we need.

What brought us joy yesterday won't be enough to bring us joy tomorrow because our emotions are shriveling and becoming numb. At first we think, "If I just had this, I would be happy." But after a while, what we desire could be coming out of our nostrils, and yet it wouldn't be enough to get our heart going anymore. We are addicted, demanding impossible levels of more and more and more.

Second, the addiction of sin also destroys us by forcing us into denial. We all know part of addiction is rationalizing our cravings and justifying doing whatever we can to meet them. We become unable to think straight and selective in our reasoning and memory—and what's more, we deny that this is even the case.

Third, sin destroys our willpower. We become addicts trying to deal with our addiction with the very thing that caused the addiction in the first place. This incident with the Israelites illustrates how sin operates like this. They longed to return to the very place they longed to be freed from: Egypt. Similarly, when we think that disobeying God will give us freedom, our freedom ends up being taken away by the very act that promised it. We may think we've placed ourselves in the driver's seat of our life, yet all we've done is allowed an addiction to take the wheel. And it gets harder and harder to resist its control.

As noted earlier, we are often in denial that sin has these effects on us. Some of you may think you aren't an addict, but there are likely a startling number of addictions in your heart that you aren't aware of. Being addicted to something may not seem like your experience, but the Bible says it is the experience of every human being to some degree. Here's why.

Recall that sin is craving something more than God and making it more important than him. God is moved to the periphery of your life, and something else takes your full focus. That object of desire, however, soon falls prey to the tolerance effect. If you think, "If I get into this career, then I'll be satisfied. I'll have what I want," what happens after you *do* get the job? It eventually pales. At first you may think, for example, "I'm a lawyer now. What a rush! I've finally arrived." A year later, however, you'll find that it's not enough. Your firm could be bigger, you could have more clients, your working hours could be better, and so on and so forth. What thrilled you at the beginning won't be enough to truly satisfy you anymore.

Or say you've always wanted to marry someone good-looking and sharp, and you finally find someone who fits the description. At first it feels like a dream. After a while, though, the tolerance effect brings you back to reality. Your spouse, much as you may love them, will never be enough to truly fulfill your hopes and dreams.

Now, you may read this and think, "What's wrong with wanting a good spouse? What's wrong with wanting a successful career? I thought you were talking about sin."

Don't you see? When you live for anything more than you live for God, that is a sin that creates an addiction. You will find that the more you get the object of your desire, the more you need it and the less satisfying it is. The heart, the emotions, and the mind shrivel.

Aldous Huxley, the author of *Brave New World*, was raised in a traditional Anglican home in England. After going off to college and encountering a range of new philosophical perspectives, he concluded that life had no inherent meaning. But later in life, he realized that his "philosophy of meaninglessness" was a convenient excuse, "an instrument of liberation" from Christian morality. He and his friends "objected to this morality because it interfered with our sexual freedom." In other words, he wanted there to be no God because he wanted to sleep around. The philosophy of meaninglessness was a justification for what he calls his "erotic revolt."[2] We shouldn't dare to think, he tells us, that philosophers are purely objective in their philosophical considerations.

But choosing something over God is not seen solely in wanting to satisfy sexual impulses. Say you choose to hold a grudge against somebody even though you know you're supposed to forgive. What does that do to your mind?

To hold a grudge against somebody, you first have to feel morally superior to that person. You can't see yourself as someone guilty of the same things that person has done. As a result, when you are presented with evidence that you—like the person you are holding a grudge against—are a sinner, weak and flawed, you'll screen out that evidence. You won't be able to see the truth because you can't crave vengeance while simultaneously seeing the reality of your own moral culpability.

Not only that, you'll screen out any evidence that the person you won't forgive isn't as bad as you thought they were. You will presume that any good they do is really evil. "Sure," you'll rationalize to yourself, "he did that nice thing for his mother, but his real motive was to profit from it somehow." Sin will not only destroy your emotions through the tolerance effect, but it will also destroy your mind. You will not be able to think straight.

In the end, even your will is gone. Here is how we see this unfold in this passage. In verse 4, the Israelites declare what is in their heart of hearts: "If only we had meat to eat!" This was their deepest burning desire. The phrase "if only" is the giveaway. The theologian Jonathan Edwards said that sin turns the heart into a fire.[3] The Bible also says that just as a fire has never said, so to speak, "That's enough fuel; I'm fine now,"[4] a sinful heart has never said, "I've had enough success. I've had enough love. I've had enough approval. I've had enough comfort." Oh, no. The more fuel you put into a fire, the higher it burns and the more fuel it needs to keep it going. This is the heart of the fire: the insatiable need for more that eventually consumes everything.

So how do you uncover the fire in your heart? The next time you're irritable, the next time you're dejected, the next time you're scared to death, ask yourself, "What am I telling myself would make me happy *if only* I had it?" There's an "if only" at the bottom of those feelings of irritation or dejection or fear. Whatever answer you uncover—whatever it is you say to yourself about *if only I had that*—that is what becomes your slave master. And it destroys your will.

Lies necessitate other lies. Envy necessitates more envy. Racism necessitates more racist thoughts. And on it goes with jealousy and bitterness and all else.

The things we crave become our slave masters because they burn in our hearts with this idea: if only. Thinking "Everything would be fine if only I had this" creates a suction in our life that demands more, more, and more to supposedly fix our unhappiness.

If sin enslaves, how, then, are we freed from it? How are we healed? While the passage offers few examples of how to act, it does provide a couple of very important insights to help answer these questions.

We Need an Intervention

As we see in verse 20, Moses comes to the Israelites and tells them, "You have rejected the LORD." That word of confrontation is what we need. Someone must come to us and say, "You think this thing in your life is your problem, but that's not your problem. Your real problem is that you have rejected God." We must be awakened by someone or something external to ourselves; we will never wake up on our own.

Someone must come after us and tell us the truth: God is not burning at the center of our life. And if God is not the center of our life, we're slaves and don't even know it. And there is no one more enslaved than the person who doesn't know they are.

All of the twelve-step programs know this. The person who thinks, "I have power over myself," is a powerless person, but the person who admits, "I am powerless. I need help," is receiving power for the first time.

This principle applies spiritually too. If you think, "I'm not terribly lost. I'm not horribly wicked. I'm not enslaved to my passions. I'm not powerless to do good. I'm a pretty good person," then you are powerless. But if you admit, "I let my heart burn for the things that will not satisfy me. I do not do what is right, and I need someone much bigger than me to help me change," then you have begun to be freed of slavery.

We Need to Worship God

The other insight into how to be freed is found in verse 20. The Hebrew text moves between the words "loathe" and "reject, refuse": "You will loathe the meat because you have rejected or refused me." The sense is that just as the Israelites lost their appetite for everything else, so they have lost their appetite for God.

If you're a Christian dealing with enslaving habits, it's not enough to slap yourself on the wrist and tell yourself, "Bad Christian! Stop that." It's not enough just to think, "I'm going to try harder next time." If that's all you do, you'll find yourself back at square one, sinning over and over again. Here's the answer: The real reason you keep having problems with these enslaving habits is because you don't have an appetite for something better. I'm not talking about believing in God. I'm not talking about even obeying God. I'm talking about *tasting* God. Here's what I mean.

The way to get out from under the enslaving habits—the secret to freedom from spiritual slavery—is to worship. You need deep, heartfelt worship. Worship that moves you to tears. Worship that fills you with joy. You have to sense the overwhelming greatness of who God is and what he has done for you. And this has to happen consistently. How can that possibly happen?

Here's an illustration that Kathy and I have found helpful. Let's say you go to someone you love and tell them, "Tuesday night, from 8:00 to 8:30, I want you to pour out your heart to me. Tell me what you're upset about and what you fear and all your concerns about whether you'll make it through life. Then, after all that, I'll put my hands on you and say, 'Honey, you're going to make it. I'm with you, and you're doing great.' Then you'll tell me how much that means to you. Tuesday night at 8:00!" If you were to do that, how would your loved one react?

Personal relationships don't work that way. If you're a parent, for example, and you need to work on taxes or pay the bills or take care of household chores, you have to do those tasks wherever the kids are at that time; you have to be available to them because you never know when one of them will come up to you and say, "I'm scared." The only way to get that sort of *quality* time is to create tons and tons of *quantity* time and wait for the special moment to come up.

That's the way it is with God too. You have to spend time

seeking him. You have to spend time reading his Word. You have to spend time in corporate worship. You have to. You won't get these incredible moments of weeping and glorious worship every time, of course, but the only way you'll *ever* experience them is if you give enough time for it to happen—if you're seeking him, if you're reflecting on him, if you're worshiping him, and if you're praying to him. That worship is the only thing that will replace the little fire burning in your heart that says, "If only."

You need a new fire that says, "If only I could see the Lord, if only he were close to my heart, if only I could feel him to be as great as I know him to be, if only I could sense his grace and taste its sweetness." When that's burning in your heart, you're free. You're able to tell yourself, "If I have God, who cares if that person snubbed me? Who cares if I'm thirty-five and not married yet? I'm free. I have this."

The only way that fire can burn in your heart is through worship. Worship, worship, worship. That's what creates the appetite. As Psalm 34:8 says, "Taste and see that the LORD is good." If you taste that the Lord is good, the tolerance effect is reversed. Don't you know his mercies are new every morning and nobody else's are? Everything else gets old. It ends up not being enough to satisfy you. It runs out of flavor. But the Lord gives more than enough each and every day.

Have you had this experience? Have you had a verse you've known all your life feel new? A song you've known for years paint you a picture of God's goodness in an amazing new way? God is the only master who doesn't enslave. He's the only master who forgives. He's the only one whose mercies are new every morning.

We Need a Savior

Last of all, we need somebody to truly save us once and for all—a real Moses who succeeded where the first Moses failed. Confronted with the Israelites' complaints, Moses says to God (I'm paraphrasing), "Their sins are falling on me all the time. These are sinners. They're infants. They're babies, and their sins are falling on me. I'm their spiritual leader, and I can't take it. I would rather die than bear the burden of taking them to the promised land."

Fortunately, we are told in Hebrews 3 that there's someone better than Moses who willingly died *in order* to bear the burden of our sins and take us to the promised land. This better Moses didn't say, "I'd rather die than bear the burden." He said, "I'll die and *thereby* take the burden." Jesus lost his freedom so we could be free. He was nailed to the cross so we could be sprung from our imprisonment. He was chained into the darkness so we could be free to fly, so we could run and not be weary, so we could walk and not faint.

We have our better Moses. The Israelites did not. This passage contains no instances of exemplary behavior, but the whole of the passage points to the One whose mercies are new every morning, the One who took the burden, the One whose service is perfect freedom, the One who said, in essence, "Anyone who sins is a slave of sin, but if you know the truth and continue in my truth, the truth will set you free."

A PRAYER FOR FREEDOM FROM SLAVERY

Thank you, Father, for giving us the possibility of complete freedom from our addictive sins. I ask you to give me that freedom. Meet me in my worship, and give me an appetite for you that surpasses my desires for all else. May my heart burn with the longing for you and the liberation you offer above all. Teach me to consecrate myself before the quails come, lest I die gorging myself on my desires—my heart, mind, and will dried up.

Father, the more I taste that you are good, the more I will taste that everything around me is delicious. If I put you first, I will be able to enjoy romance, success, career, and everything else without becoming a slave to them. Help me to live as your child indeed, because I have a greater Moses, the One who took all my sins. Because he was nailed to the cross, I've been freed. I thank you for this in Jesus's name. Amen.

CHAPTER 9

HEALING OF SIN: TRUE REPENTANCE

Psalm 51:1–10

[1] Have mercy on me, O God,
    according to your unfailing love;
according to your great compassion
    blot out my transgressions.
[2] Wash away all my iniquity
    and cleanse me from my sin.
[3] For I know my transgressions,
    and my sin is always before me.
[4] Against you, you only, have I sinned

and done what is evil in your sight,
so that you are proved right when you speak
and justified when you judge.
[5] Surely I was sinful at birth,
sinful from the time my mother
conceived me.
[6] Surely you desire truth in the inner parts;
you teach me wisdom in the inmost place.
[7] Cleanse me with hyssop, and I will be clean;
wash me, and I will be whiter than snow.
[8] Let me hear joy and gladness;
let the bones you have crushed rejoice.
[9] Hide your face from my sins
and blot out all my iniquity.
[10] Create in me a pure heart, O God,
and renew a steadfast spirit within me.

I once heard somebody say, "You know, in the end, people don't really change." When I heard that, my blood curdled. That statement is as much a denial of the gospel—of the essential Christian message—as is asserting, "Jesus isn't who he said he was, God himself." In this chapter, we'll look at the most profound change any human being can undergo—the healing of sin—and at how it is accomplished. In 1970 I crossed over from a life simply following religion to finding real faith in Jesus, but for at least three years after that, very few, if any, changes occurred in my life that the Bible says should have been there. I continued to struggle with thoughts and habits and feelings that just wouldn't budge.

Then I started seminary, training for ministry. During the first semester, I took a course in which I had to read some old writings. A couple of them were on what the old writers used to call "mortification," which is a fancy, antique word for repentance. As I read those old writings, I realized my problem was I did not know how to repent.

The reason I didn't know how to repent was the same reason most people still don't know how to repent: We think we already know. And if we think we already know how to do something, we rarely try to learn how to do it. Almost nobody takes a class on how to breathe, for example, and for the same reason, few of us study how to repent. We think, "Repentance. Of course. If I do something wrong, I repent. I'm sorrowful. I say I'm sorry." But unless and until you understand true repentance, the gospel will remain only an implicit, untapped power in your life. The changes you want, the changes you seek, the changes you need—the secret to all of it is repentance.

Psalm 51 is perhaps the greatest passage in the Bible on the theme of repentance, and by examining it we discover the key to being healed of our sin. First, we must connect the psalm to the historical incident that instigated its writing. This is a psalm of David, and the context for it can be found in 2 Samuel 11–12. More briefly, you can consult the heading for the psalm, placed in most editions of the Bible, that tells readers the circumstances under which the psalm was written.

The caption for Psalm 51 in my Bible reads, "A psalm of David. When the prophet Nathan came to him after David had committed adultery with Bathsheba." The story is well-known. Uriah the Hittite was one of David's truest and best friends, one of the thirty-seven men who went out into the wilderness with David when Saul was trying to kill him (2 Samuel 23:39). They risked everything to protect David, who would certainly have been killed without them. David owed Uriah and those men his life.

Uriah was a great soldier and, at the time of the events leading to the creation of this psalm, had been out fighting against the Ammonites in Israel's army. David, the king, had remained in Jerusalem and saw Uriah's wife, Bathsheba, and desired her. After he had an affair with her, she became pregnant, which was a problem, of course, because her husband was away on a military campaign. So in an attempt to cover up what he had done, David called Uriah back from the front, ostensibly to learn how the battle was going but secretly to goad Uriah into making love to his wife so he would never suspect any infidelity.

David listened to Uriah's report, making sure to ask enough questions so that they were there until late in the day. Then, once enough time had passed, David told Uriah to stay overnight before going back to the front, urging him to go home, relax, have a great meal, take a bath, and have sex with his wife.

But Uriah refused, telling David, "The ark and Israel and

Judah are staying in tents, and my master Joab and my lord's men are camped in the open fields. How could I go to my house to eat and drink and lie with my wife? As surely as you live, I will not do such a thing!" (2 Samuel 11:11).

The earnestness and integrity of Uriah is remarkable, isn't it? But because Uriah didn't go into his home, David had a problem. So David sent a message to his general, Joab: "Put Uriah in the front line where the fighting is fiercest. Then withdraw from him so he will be struck down and die" (v. 15).

Joab obeyed. As soon as Uriah was killed, Bathsheba went into mourning.

After the time of mourning was over, David married her, and she gave birth to the child. David thought everything was fine. But Nathan the prophet came and gave one of the greatest sermons in the history of the world. Nathan said to David,

> "There were two men in a certain town, one rich and the other poor. The rich man had a very large number of sheep and cattle, but the poor man had nothing except one little ewe lamb he had bought. He raised it, and it grew up with him and his children. It shared his food, drank from his cup and even slept in his arms. It was like a daughter to him.
>
> "Now a traveler came to the rich man, but the rich man refrained from taking one of his own sheep or cattle

to prepare a meal for the traveler who had come to him. Instead, he took the ewe lamb that belonged to the poor man and prepared it for the one who had come to him." (2 Samuel 12:1–4)

The text tells us that David "burned with anger" and said to Nathan, "As surely as the LORD lives, the man who did this deserves to die! He must pay for that lamb four times over, because he did such a thing and had no pity" (vv. 5–6). *This is a heartless man!*, David said. *Does he think there's no justice in the kingdom? Let him stand before the king. Who is this man?*

Nathan told him, "You are the man!" (v. 7). It's the most devastating sermon application in the history of the world.

Before we examine the effect of this sermon on David, let me encourage you to thank God for the Nathans in your life. We would be dead without people who bring the Word of God to us and lay it on our hearts, because without them we are unable to do what the Word tells us. I've been fortunate enough to marry one of my Nathans. Do you have Nathans in your life? Do you *let them* be Nathans? Are you a Nathan to anybody else? Even the Nathans wouldn't be Nathans unless they had Nathans. We should be thankful for them—though usually we don't feel thankful until a year or two after they do their work.

Upon hearing Nathan's rebuke, David was devastated and plunged into the darkest despair. Everything he had was hanging by a thread. He had blown up his life. How could he continue to be a king in light of all he had done? How could he ever look at himself in the mirror, let alone face God again? How was he going to keep from killing himself?

In Psalm 51 we have an account of how he got out of these greatest depths of despair. And he didn't just get out; he triumphed. He became a greater leader and a greater man of God than before. How is that possible after such a disaster? Because he repented. Maybe you're thinking, "I don't understand that. Whenever I repent, I feel even worse, like I'm dirty, polluted, and weak. How could David end up better off than before?"

It is a remarkable turn. In the next chapter we'll examine it further, but I'll simply note here that David comes out of this singing. Psalm 51:14–15 says,

> My tongue will sing of your righteousness.
> O Lord, open my lips,
>   and my mouth will declare your praise.

Notice how he's not even singing about God's mercy; he is singing of God's righteousness. How did David get to the place where the holiness and righteousness of God is now a comfort to him? Where did he get this kind of boldness? Repentance.

The first thing this story tells us is we all desperately need repentance. What do I mean by that? After all, most of us haven't covered up an affair by committing a murder. But that's missing the point.

David was one of the great people of history. David was the main prototype in the Bible for Jesus himself. The Messiah is called the Son of David. Why? Because David had it all together. He was an artist. He was a poet. He was a musician whose works have lasted for centuries. He was a great leader, a brave warrior, and a beloved of the Lord. There had never been a greater man than David.

Here is the question this raises: If even the great David had sin in his heart, do we think we're too good not to? If David was capable of what he did, aren't we all? If David, through a lack of repentance, had unaddressed things in his heart that finally exploded and blew up his life, shouldn't we think *we* have them as well? We need repentance too.

The power of repentance is amazing. Throughout my years as a pastor, I've listened to people describe how they messed up their lives, but I'm not sure any of those stories were worse than what David did. And yet even he triumphed.

For that to happen, however, all the elements of repentance had to be there. The same is true for us today. If you find that repentance has brought you a sense of guilt and dread instead of joy, if you find yourself falling back into the same old things over and over again instead of actually being changed, you haven't truly repented. You either haven't done it yet, haven't done it properly, or haven't done it purely.

If you want to know how to repent well, look at four elements of proper repentance that can be found in verse 4:

Against you, you only, have I sinned
and done what is evil in your sight,
so that you are proved right when you speak
and justified when you judge.

The way the Puritans used to identify the four principles of repentance was by saying you have to see your sin, you have to confess your sin, you have to mourn your sin, and you have to hate your sin.[1] You have to see, confess, mourn, and hate.

The first two—seeing and confessing sin—are intellectual, cognitive matters. They are disciplines that, in many ways, have nothing to do with feelings. They require us to think. Then, if you do the first two right, the second two— mourning and hating sin—will bring about an earthquake in your life: a powerful shaking up of your emotions that results in a transformed life.

Seeing Your Sin

The first principle—seeing your sin—is revealed by David's assertion that he has sinned and done what is evil in God's sight. This is a cognitive action. The first step of repentance is educating your conscience with the truth, the law, and the Word of God so you can be sure your guilt is genuine and proportional. You have to see your sin as it really is. The only way to do that is to see it as God sees it.

This is important and not as simple as it may seem. We must be careful not to view sin from any perspective other than God's. Don't see your sin according to the way your mother or your father sees it. Don't see it according to the way your friends see it. Don't tell yourself, subtly or unconsciously, "I have sinned in Dad's sight. I have sinned in my friends' sight. I have sinned in *The New York Times* op-ed page's sight." Be careful, even, of thinking, "I have sinned in my feelings' sight."

In our era it is a fairly common approach to think, "I have sinned in my sight. I haven't lived up to my own standards." But who cares about your standards? Repentance is necessary when we fall short of *God's* standards. This is why David not only refuses to let anyone else judge him but also refuses to judge himself. He acknowledges that he has sinned *in God's sight*.

Think back to the story in chapter 7 about Rebecca Pippert and her psychology course. When Pippert asked her professor how a patient's dilemma should be solved, he told her that psychology can't give someone the ability to forgive others, nor can it give them the ability to receive forgiveness. Psychology, despite all its benefits, ultimately can't deal with guilt. As noted earlier, psychology is science, and science can only tell you what actually is—how people learn, respond, operate, and so on. Science can tell you what *is*, but it can never tell you what *ought to be*. If you are facing guilt of any sort, no secular, scientific method will give you a proper way to deal with that guilt. Instead, the only way you can truly begin to handle your guilt is by asking, "Is this true guilt? Should I feel guilty, or should I not? Is it disproportional? Is it something I've really done wrong, or do I just think I've done wrong?"

When a counselor directly states or indirectly suggests (as often happens) that you shouldn't feel guilty about something, the counselor is not practicing science. They are practicing religion. The minute someone makes a claim that "This is right; this is wrong. You're feeling too guilty about this," they've entered the realm of moral standards. And moral standards are matters of reasoning and of faith.

When you process your guilt, there's no way around asking yourself, "What is absolutely right and absolutely wrong?" And you can't look inside yourself to determine those universal absolutes. You can't look at your own feelings. The conscience is like a faulty smoke alarm. The smoke alarms in my apartment building go off if you so much as strike a match. You light one candle and suddenly they're screaming at you even though there's no danger. Other smoke alarms won't go off until they detect a burning body.

A smoke alarm has to be rightly calibrated in order to function properly. So do consciences. Some consciences send people into suicidal despair over small, inconsequential things—things their culture or parents or friends told them were wrong, even if those things aren't wrong according to their own standards. Other people have consciences that always warn that they're failing to live up to their own exacting standards, even when the rest of the world thinks they're doing great. And still other people have consciences that fail to go off for all but the most grievous offenses. How do you know if what you've done is truly wrong? You can't determine that by looking at your conscience.

Don't you see there is no secular answer for guilt? You have to determine what is right and wrong apart from just looking to your heart. You have to *educate* your heart. You have to ask, "How does God see this?" And the only way to determine that is by examining the moral law of God in the Bible. It's the only way. You have to see your sin as God sees it. Have you sinned *in his sight*?

Confessing Your Sin

The second part of true repentance is to confess your sin. You have to take responsibility. David does that, admitting that he has "sinned and done what is evil" (v. 4). David had to take responsibility because it was his sin that caused the state he was in.

This whole book has been an attempt to answer the question, What is wrong with the world? How is it possible for human beings to do the terrible things they do? The answer of every chapter is that it is possible because of the sin in our hearts. But let's get a little bit closer to the bone. Ninety-nine percent of the time, we don't do horrible things because we said, "Hey, let's get up and go do something wicked." No, we are able to do horrible things because we find ways to avoid taking responsibility for them.

We see this in every war, every conflict. One side is confronted with an atrocity committed, and the response is to point to what the other side did.

Over and over again, we say, "Well, maybe what I'm doing is wrong, but . . ." Eve says, "Maybe what I did was wrong, but the serpent . . ." Adam says, "Maybe what I did was wrong, but Eve . . ." We find a way of saying, "I'm not responsible. It's the other person's fault." Even David responds this way after he has Uriah killed. He sends Joab a message that says, "Don't let this upset you; the sword devours one as well as another" (2 Samuel 11:25). In other words, "The Ammonites did it."

But he didn't just say it in the message to Joab. There's indication all throughout 2 Samuel 11–12 that he also said it in his heart, telling himself things like, "My needs are bigger than the rules. I suffer under a king's responsibilities. I've made so many sacrifices. God doesn't want me to live a miserable life. My responsibilities go beyond those that other people have to shoulder, so my comforts need to as well." Every man I've ever talked to who had committed adultery told himself some variation of these justifications.

I'm sure you have heard all the excuses. And I expect that you've offered some yourself. Do you realize that whenever you say, "Maybe this is wrong, but . . ." you are using the very same logic that enabled all the worst atrocities in history? There is no way out of your sin unless you take full responsibility.

When Nathan appears before David and says, "You are the man!" he goes on to say, "You killed him with the sword of the Ammonites" (2 Samuel 12:9). When David repents, he does not continue to justify his actions. He throws away the excuses and admits, *It's my sin. I'm the one who sinned.*

Years ago I heard somebody put it this way: Imagine you see a log on the ground and need to throw it somewhere else. If all you do is pick up one end of the log while the other is still on the ground, you won't be able to throw it anywhere. But if you grab the log in the middle, pick it up, and put the whole weight on yourself, you can toss it away. Unless you take the weight fully on, you'll never be able to take it fully off.

You must be willing to tell yourself, "My circumstances may have mistreated me and provided the *occasion* for my sin but were not the *cause* of my sin. I wanted to do it. And I did it. The reason I'm miserable today is not because of my circumstances; it's because of my response to my circumstances. I wanted to do it. I have sinned."

What's more, you have to see that the very fact you have not taken full responsibility is the very reason you're in the place you are now.

Many people go to God and think they've repented, but all they've really done is complain about the circumstances around the sin. They haven't accepted responsibility for their sin, and that's the reason they're in the situation they're in. Unless you take it fully on, you'll never be able to take it fully off.

Mourning Your Sin

The third step necessary for repentance is to mourn your sin. David says to God, "Against you, you only, have I sinned" (Psalm 51:4). Do you notice the doubling language? He doesn't just say, "You only." He says, "You, you." In the Semitic languages, one effective way to get across intensity of emotion is repetition. So, for example, when his beloved son dies, David cries, "O my son Absalom! O Absalom, my son, my son!" (2 Samuel 19:4.) The repetition is a reflection of intense emotion. Here, in the psalm, he says, "Against you, you only." The repetition expresses his deep sorrow for, his mourning over, his sin.

Now, there seems to be a big problem with this "only." Someone can read this and understandably object. After all, at a minimum, David sinned against Uriah, to say nothing of Bathsheba or Joab. How could David say he sinned only against God?

There's a good theological answer to that question; but more than just the answer is at stake here. First, though, the answer: The reason it's a sin to harm another person, according to the Bible, is because that other person is made in the image of God, is owned by God, and has dignity placed on them by God. That's why harming another person is wrong.

If, however, you believe there is no Creator who made us and that we're all accidents of nature, I defy you to give a rational basis for the value of human life. Give me a reason for the difference in moral value between a human being and a rock. You might think, "Well, everybody knows a human being is more valuable than a rock." Sure. We know the truth on an emotional and intuitive level. But is there a rational basis for that belief?

If there is no God, what's wrong with harming somebody else? Why is cutting down a person any worse than cutting down a tree? Aren't they both, in this view, simply entities created randomly by an accident of the universe?

Now, that reality—that people's value lies in being created by God in his image—is the reason it's legitimate to say that if any sin isn't against God first, it isn't a sin against him at all. But that's not really what David is saying. If he was simply trying to make a theologically correct statement, he'd have said, "Against you, you primarily, have I sinned." But instead, he says, "Against you, you only."

Here's why. Everyone knows you can't remove a tumor without being cut open. In the same way, you can't repent without metaphorically cutting yourself open to remove the sin. Here, David is making an incision into his heart. And what is he making it with? Look at verse 1. There he says,

Have mercy on me, O God,
according to your unfailing love;
according to your great compassion
blot out my transgressions.

David is confessing that his sin is ultimately the betrayal of a good and loving God. He wounds himself, he makes an incision in his heart, by showing himself the goodness and the grace of God. Crucially, he doesn't do so by looking at the law and thinking, "If I don't obey, I'm going to be punished." And that difference makes all the difference.

Repenting with a punishment mindset is really just a way of using God, because what you're really saying is, "I'd better obey or I won't get what I want." In contrast, David's posture is, *What makes this wrong is not simply that I broke a rule, but rather that I broke God's heart. The problem is not just that I trampled on his law, but that I trampled on him. I need to repent not to get what I want but to stop trampling on the very loveliness of God. I have grieved a good friend, someone whose love is unfailing, someone whose compassion is infinite.* David is mourning his sin. Only this approach will change you, and it's crucial to understand why. Your life could depend on it.

When living in fear of punishment, you may find your sin restrained for a time, but your heart will not be transformed. You will never experience true change if you simply say to God, "Lord, I was bad because I committed adultery. I broke the seventh commandment, so I know you're going to punish me. Oh Lord, please have mercy on me." With that approach, you may end up hating yourself, but you will not end up hating your sin.

By contrast, look at David's attitude: *Lord, I see that I've trampled on you, and I don't care what the consequences are. You are just in your judging. What I want is to love you and honor you and be right with you again.* This is the kind of repentance that focuses on God and makes him the end you are seeking. This approach, in contrast to the other, will make you hate your sin without making you hate yourself.

Why? What makes the difference? It's the unwavering assurance that God loves him—that's what convicts David so profoundly. So it is with us. The assurance that you mean the world to God—the assurance of your value—is what convicts you into the ground. As a result, you come to hate the sin, the thing that has trampled on his loveliness, while still holding on to your sense of value and worth.

Hating Your Sin

Finally, if you have done the first three steps correctly, you will change no matter what the consequences of your sin are. You won't care if God allows other challenges to unfold in your life, because you'll know that the important thing is that you're going to change.

If you have seen your sin, confessed your sin, and mourned

your sin, your heart will be cleansed with a hatred of sin but not of yourself. And you will find permanent changes coming. You'll be able to say, "Lord, I would love it if you got rid of the mess I have created in my life, but that doesn't matter. What matters is that I know you love me, that I love you, and that we have fellowship again." Hating your sin means you really do change.

Jesus Christ shows us how to do this. Jesus lived a sinless life, so he never needed to repent, but he did show us that the way up really is down. The world says Clark Kent has to become Superman to save the world. The gospel says Superman had to become Clark Kent to save the world. What looks like the path to your destruction—stripping away your self-righteousness and admitting you are a sinner—is actually the way to resurrection.

We follow Jesus because he's the One who taught us that the repenting soul is the triumphant soul, that to lose our lives is to find our lives, that we behold his grace and glory in the dark valley, not on the mountaintop. Let us find his light in our darkness, his joy in our sorrow, his grace in our sin, and his riches in our poverty. This is the way to be healed of our sin.

A PRAYER FOR TRUE REPENTANCE

Father, I thank you that it's possible to know your grace and glory in the valley. Help me see what I should be doing. Teach me how to go to your Word to see how to live, but then to the cross to see how Jesus succeeded for me where I've failed. Educate my heart with your truth, then help me to turn and see your unfailing love in Jesus dying for us. Let me be so moved that I not only see and confess my sin but mourn and hate it too.

We have the resources to see your mercy and forgiveness in a way David did not. Help me to be so wounded by your love that I find myself utterly and completely healed. Open my lips and let them show forth thy praise. In Jesus's name I pray. Amen.

CHAPTER 10

HEALING OF SIN: INTIMACY WITH GOD

Psalm 51

[1] Have mercy on me, O God,
    according to your unfailing love;
according to your great compassion
    blot out my transgressions.
[2] Wash away all my iniquity
    and cleanse me from my sin.
[3] For I know my transgressions,
    and my sin is always before me.

⁴ Against you, you only, have I sinned
  and done what is evil in your sight,
so that you are proved right when you speak
  and justified when you judge.
⁵ Surely I was sinful at birth,
  sinful from the time my mother
    conceived me.
⁶ Surely you desire truth in the inner parts;
  you teach me wisdom in the inmost place.
⁷ Cleanse me with hyssop, and I will be clean;
  wash me, and I will be whiter than snow.
⁸ Let me hear joy and gladness;
  let the bones you have crushed rejoice.
⁹ Hide your face from my sins
  and blot out all my iniquity.
¹⁰ Create in me a pure heart, O God,
  and renew a steadfast spirit within me.
¹¹ Do not cast me from your presence
  or take your Holy Spirit from me.
¹² Restore to me the joy of your salvation
  and grant me a willing spirit, to sustain me.
¹³ Then I will teach transgressors your ways,
  and sinners will turn back to you.
¹⁴ Save me from bloodguilt, O God,
  the God who saves me,
  and my tongue will sing of your
    righteousness.

^{15} O Lord, open my lips,
   and my mouth will declare your praise.
^{16} You do not delight in sacrifice, or I would bring
      it;
   you do not take pleasure in burnt offerings.
^{17} The sacrifices of God are a broken spirit;
   a broken and contrite heart,
   O God, you will not despise.
^{18} In your good pleasure make Zion prosper;
   build up the walls of Jerusalem.
^{19} Then there will be righteous sacrifices,
   whole burnt offerings to delight you;
   then bulls will be offered on your altar.

P salm 51 says something to everybody. We have already seen that it gives hope to people who have blown up their lives by doing something foolish and wrong and are experiencing the consequences of that foolishness.

The psalm also addresses people who think, "This is fine for David, but it isn't for me. This is for people who *really* screw up. It's not like I couldn't make a huge mistake, I suppose, but I'm not going to. And I haven't. So while it's great for people who have really screwed up, it's not for me." That is a dangerous line of thought. David the beloved, the man close to God's heart, one of the godliest and greatest figures in the history of the world, was capable of life-exploding sin. And so are we. David needed repentance, and so do we.

Here's what sin does: It plants land mines all throughout your life. Maybe yours haven't blown up yet. That's great. But they will blow up if you don't deal with them. Repentance is the process of minesweeping your own heart. If you think you don't need to sweep for mines, you are almost guaranteeing that your life will blow up.

But Psalm 51 also speaks to a third group of people: those of us in the middle of those two positions. We're the people who acknowledge that there are things wrong with us, that we have things that could blow up our life. We know we need to change, and we're trying to work on them. We're trying to sweep for mines. Yet it seems like we never truly unearth them. We never truly fix the problem. We get upset about these sins and sorry about them, especially when they cause little eruptions and create problems for us. When that occurs, we think we repent. We stop sinning for a while, but the next thing we know, we're back doing it again. We never change.

If that describes you—if you are in this third group— Psalm 51 is for you too. It tells you how to change permanently, how to truly repent. In the previous chapter, we noted that this repentance involves seeing, confessing, mourning, and hating your sin. Now let's take a deeper look at what we can learn from David's repentance.

Cutting Yourself Open

As mentioned earlier, repentance means cutting ourselves open to get the malignant growth of sin out—and cutting deep, deep down to extract it. If we find ourselves persisting in sin without any change, we likely aren't cutting all the way. We must imitate two things that David does to cut himself deep enough.

Seeing Sin as God Sees It

First, he makes sure he begins by seeing sin the way God sees it. He insists on it. We see this in verse 4, where he says, "Against you, you only, have I sinned and done what is evil in your sight." Perhaps the most confounding problem humans have is our ability to do evil because we find a way to view it as good. By way of illustration, most of us have a favorite photograph of ourselves. Why is it our favorite? Because it hides our flaws. Those of us with big noses, for example, know that if we take a picture from just the right angle, we can make the nose look less prominent. With the camera at just the right point of view, the size of the nose diminishes and the face looks wonderful. We can always find a point of view that hides reality.

This is why one ethnic group can wage open war on another ethnic group and argue, "They did something worse to us two hundred years ago. When you look at things from a historical perspective, what we're doing isn't so bad." As we saw in the last chapter, this is what David did after the killing of Uriah, saying, in essence, "From a certain point of view, I didn't really kill Uriah. It was the Ammonites. It was the war that killed him, not me."

But take a moment to realize what this behavior means. If we go to these lengths to justify any sins in our lives, we can end up doing it to justify atrocities we previously never could've imagined. Human beings have justified anything and everything throughout history—because we can always find a way to look at something that makes it seem not so bad.

This is especially true in the late modern Western cultures that profess every point of view to be of equal value. In many college classrooms in New York City and elsewhere, students are told that all points of view are valid. Regardless of what somebody holds to be true or right in their eyes, the rest of us are encouraged to affirm their worldview and acknowledge it as legitimate. But if you operate on this principle, it becomes exceptionally easy to justify the most horrible of actions to yourself. After all, it's your point of view, is it not? If your point of view is equally as valid as everyone else's, then whatever you're doing isn't so bad and you're not really doing anything wrong, right?

If there is no ultimate point of view, one that is above our own individual preferences and perspectives, there is absolutely no way at all to deal with the sins and the problems and the evils of life. You can kiss the idea of justice goodbye. You can stop all your meetings and commissions and elections where somebody says, "I have the answer!"

We have to have a single point of view that stands apart from our individual ones, one that actually sees things as they are and knows how to deal with them. David found it. Rather than using a flawed, human understanding that leads to messing up again and again, David looked at his sins the way God looks at them.

Throwing Away the Excuses

The second thing David does, which we touched on in the last chapter, is take full responsibility for his actions. He throws away the excuses. In verses 1 and 2, he refers to what he's done as his "transgression" and "iniquity," both of which indicate deliberate rebellion. Most interesting is that in verse 6 he says, "Surely you desire truth in the inner parts."

What he is saying is this: "I sinned because I wanted to. I freely chose it, and I take full responsibility. I make no excuses. I can't blame the pressures of being a king. I can't blame Bathsheba. I can't blame anybody. I can't blame anything. I take all the blame on myself. There wasn't truth in my inner self, as God wanted—just my own desire."

The same is true for us. When we sin, it's not because of our circumstances. It's not because of someone else's actions. It's because of what's inside us—our inner parts. We wanted to do it.[1]

Here's how this works itself out in our own lives. We find ourselves saying things like, "I didn't want to lie, but if I had told the truth, I would have lost my job. Circumstances forced me to lie." What would David say in response? "What you really mean is you did it because at that moment you wanted money and security more than you wanted to demonstrate honesty, please God, and help the people who needed the truth. You did it because you wanted to do it."

Don't ever, ever, tell yourself, "Circumstances made me do it." Circumstances might shape our sin, but they never cause our sin. Sin is always and only caused by our own inner desires.

We shouldn't dare blame anybody or anything for our own failure. The temptations, the mistreatment, the things people do to us will undoubtedly change the specifics of our sin. But they don't give birth to the sin. The sin is birthed in our own hearts.

Failure to realize this is what leads to false repentance, to little more than complaining. We tell God, "I'm sorry for what happened. But my parents did this to me. My stress level did this. I was so tired. My wife did this. My husband did this," and then we tell ourselves we've repented. And yet we still feel bad about what we did, and we even do it again. Unless we cut all the way to our core, we can't fully remove the sin.

Now, after the incision is made, how do we *actually* remove sin from our hearts?

Removing Sin

Look to David, who does two things. First, he softens and melts his heart by taking it to the grace of God. (Stay with me: I'm about to mix my metaphors. I know I've been referring to surgery and now I'm going to refer to blacksmithing, but I have to do it.) If you have a metallic object that's cracked, you can't fix it just by hitting it with a hammer. Doing so will only dent the outside of whatever you're attempting to repair or break it even more. But it won't fix the fracture. By the same token, there is a way of convicting yourself of sin that is so self-flagellating that it ends up only making you feel worse. That's not the idea. Instead of smashing our hearts to pieces like this, we need to reshape them. As we saw in the last chapter, Jonathan Edwards says that true repentance *does* involve a kind of violence, but it's the violence of a flame.

Softening Your Heart

A metallic object must be repaired by heating it up and melting it down because that's the only way you can reshape it and make it whole again. In the same way, instead of hammering his heart, David offers it to the grace and the covenant mercies of God. He doesn't wound himself with the *fear* of God. He does so with the *mercy* of God. As the seventeenth-century English clergyman Stephen Charnock puts it, David doesn't make himself miserable through fear; he makes himself miserable through mercy.[2] Right away in verse 1, David says he's going to God "according to [his] unfailing love."

The Hebrew word translated into "unfailing love" is one of the most important words in the Bible. We talked about this earlier in the book. The word is impossible to translate in one or even two words and still get the full sentiment across. "Unfailing love" is about as good as we've got in English, but it's not enough. *Chesed* means God's promised love, his covenant love, his love under oath, his unbending, unbreakable, permanent love. You can't understand the Bible without this word.

When David begins his repentance by filling his mind with the unfailing love of God, he is thinking about all the most incredible and inexplicable events in the history of Israel. He's thinking about places where God has bound himself to be loving and gracious to his people no matter what. For example, David is probably thinking of the events of Exodus 32, in which the Israelites—whom God had rescued from Egypt and to whom he'd given so much—turn away from the Lord and start worshiping a golden calf. God says to Moses, "Now leave me alone so that my anger may burn against them and that I may destroy them. Then I will make you into a great nation" (Exodus 32:10). Put another way, he is saying, "Let me go. Free me."

I want to be careful here. When God talks, he's trying to teach. And what he's trying to teach both Moses and us here is *not* that he makes mistakes or changes his mind. Since

God knows everything, he can't change his mind. You can change your mind only if you get new information. Instead, he's speaking in this way to get a point across. He's trying to say to Moses, "In spite of my justice and in spite of what the Israelites have done, I am bound to them by my oath. I have bound my heart to them. I want you to leave me alone, to free me. I want to let them go, but I can't." Isn't this strange? What he wants us to realize is this: *God has bound himself to love us. He has limited his unlimitedness.*

We can understand this even better if we connect this passage in Exodus 32 with a passage in Genesis 15. David was almost certainly also thinking about Genesis 15. There Abraham sees God pass between pieces of dead animals, and God tells him that though he is a just God, and though Abraham and the Israelites are going to fail, he will bless him and his spiritual descendants no matter the cost. God knows exactly what the Israelites are going to do in Exodus 32. And yet he will find a way to save them anyway, even if it means being cut up like these animals. Genesis 15 makes Exodus 32 explicable. But what makes Genesis 15 understandable?

The answer is available to us in ways it wasn't to David. You can see something David couldn't see. You can recast your heart in a fire that's brighter and more brilliant and more wonderful than anything David had. You can see Jesus Christ in the garden and on the cross. You can see God saying to Jesus, in effect, "Son, I'm going to tell you something I've never told anyone, and I will never say it again. Throughout all eternity I've always said and always will say, 'If you obey me, I'll come near to you.' But to you I say, 'If you obey me now, I will abandon you.' I will let *you* go, so I don't have to let *them* go. I will pour all the wrath and punishment humanity's sins deserve onto you. And even though you are the eternal Son of God, the pain and the power of that justice will be so great, your body and soul will be ripped apart—so theirs don't have to be. Are you willing to do this?"

Jesus said, "Yes."

That's unfailing love.

Why does David fill his heart with God's unfailing love? How could that transform him? When David looks at this unfailing love and this (to him) inexplicable, incredible fact that the holy and just God has somehow bound himself to be gracious to us no matter what, no matter the cost, it reveals to David why he sinned in the first place. Because he had lost his first love.

You have to cut all the way down to get the tumor out. Repenting solely from a fear of punishment and saying, "O Lord, I need to obey you or you're going to reject me," doesn't get under the tumor. David's repentant attitude says this: *Why was there an incredible pull in my heart toward Bathsheba? Why was I willing to murder for her? Because before I committed physical adultery, I had already committed spiritual adultery.*

When he says in Psalm 51:12, "Restore to me the joy of your salvation," we tend to think, "Oh, he lost the joy of his salvation because he sinned." That's true, but that's not all. There is more to it. He sinned *because* he lost the joy of his salvation. We only ever sin because we've lost the joy of our salvation. David forgot God's unfailing love. He wasn't ravished by it deep in his heart.

In Psalm 51 he sees that the reason he sinned against Uriah and Bathsheba was because he stopped being excited by God. He stopped enjoying him. He stopped being moved by his unfailing love and sacrifice. Until we see that we sin for the same reasons, we won't cut ourselves deep enough to remove our sin. We'll never truly repent.

But if you are able to repent like David—if you say, "Lord, I stand before you—not out of a fear of punishment but because I know you would be cut to pieces rather than reject me"—then you see something. You see that the very thing that convicts you of sin also shows you how valuable you are. As we have said earlier, you don't hate yourself; you hate the sin.

If you see what he did for you, how much he values you, you'll hate the sin itself, and the sin will start to lose its power over you.

Why? Because you'll say, "I lost sight of you, God, before I ever sinned. What beauty is like your beauty? Whose approval is like your approval? What love is like your love? Nobody's—and yet I was looking somewhere else." This is what it means to make ourselves miserable with mercy, to cut all the way down, and to melt our hearts—not by dwelling on how much we sinned against God's law and provoked his wrath but by reflecting on how deeply we sinned against his grace.

As a result, we forsake our sin and can have a completely changed life. We see our sin ("In your sight"), we admit our sin ("I take full responsibility"), we melt our heart down and grieve and mourn over the sin underneath the sin, which is a trampling on the grace of God and the loss of the joy of our salvation, and then we forsake sin.

Forsaking Sin

How do we know whether we did the first three steps right? We experience the fourth. In verses 1–9, we see David go through the first three. Then, from verse 10 onward, we see him create a whole new life. It's a life of obedience: "Renew a steadfast spirit within me" (v. 10). It's a life of intimacy with God: "Do not cast me from your presence or take your Holy Spirit from me" (v. 11). It's a life of continual repentance: "The sacrifices of God are a broken spirit; a broken and contrite heart, O God, you will not despise" (v. 17). Repentance is not reserved for isolated, demoralizing events or for when we blow up our lives. Repentance is a regular, lifelong practice. As John Newton put it,

> With pleasing grief and mournful joy,
> My spirit now is fill'd,
> That I should such a life destroy,
> Yet live by Him I killed.[3]

Think about this phrase: the "pleasing grief" of continually repenting. Imagine David's internal monologue: "When I do something bad, I repent. When I do something good, I'm going to repent again. I'm going to say, 'Do you think, oh foolish heart, that you accomplished that? That was a gift of grace.'" If we adopt this practice in our own lives, it softens us. When you're proud, repent and it'll bring you *down* and back to God. When you're unhappy and you've failed, repent and it'll bring you *up* and back to God. As Martin Luther tells us in the first of his Ninety-Five Theses, Jesus "willed the entire life of believers to be one of repentance."⁴ All of life is repentance.

David has found a life of obedience, a life of repentance, a life of intimacy with God, and a life of usefulness. Now he chooses to sing about God's grace and change the world. And you know what? The consequences of what he had done did not vanish. His family life became a mess for the rest of his days, full of favoritism, division, and jealousy. His sin resulted in a tremendous fallout. Yet of all the children David had, why did God choose Solomon, the child of David and Bathsheba, to be the joy of David's life and the one who carried on the messianic line? Why is it that David and Bathsheba, still called Uriah's wife, are in the genealogy of Jesus in Matthew 1?

It's God's way of telling us, "If you sin, my dear children, there will be consequences, maybe far-reaching ones. But you are never, ever, ever moved to plan B. I am so wise and so sovereign, and I love you so much that I will weave even your failures into plan A. I will continue to work through you—even in greater ways than before—after your sin. Don't you dare sin. It wrongs me, and it will hurt you, and there will be consequences. But at the same time, don't you dare think you can ever destroy my plan for your life. There is no plan B."

As the Westminster Confession of Faith puts it, "As there is no sin so small but it deserves damnation; so there is no sin so great that it can bring damnation upon those who truly repent."[5] In response to that, how can we not say with David,

> "My tongue will sing of your righteousness.
> O Lord, open my lips,
> and my mouth will declare your praise."
> (Psalm 51:14–15)

A PRAYER FOR INTIMACY WITH GOD

Lord, may my mind be filled with this vision of true repentance. May I dedicate myself to cutting the sin out of my heart because of the wonderful sacrifice you have made for me. Help me to remember that you satisfy in ways that sin and the things of this world never could. Your love is better than any other I could crave. Your affirmation, your attention, and your comfort are the most complete versions of these blessings that I could ever receive. Help me know that you are more than enough every day. Recast my heart so that I may not sin against you, not out of a spirit of fear or punishment but out of an appreciation for your love. May I, like David, find a life of obedience and intimacy with you. In Jesus's name. Amen.

NOTES

INTRODUCTION

1. Andrew Delbanco, *The Death of Satan: How Americans Have Lost the Sense of Evil* (New York: Farrar, Straus and Giroux, 1995), 3.
2. Delbanco, *Death of Satan*, 3.
3. Delbanco, *Death of Satan*, 3.
4. Thomas Harris, *The Silence of the Lambs* (New York: St. Martin's, 1988), 21, quoted in Delbanco, *The Death of Satan*, 19.
5. Fyodor Dostoevsky, *The Brothers Karamazov*, trans. Constance Garnett (New York: Random House, 1993, originally 1880), 245–46.
6. Dorothy Sayers, *Christian Letters to a Post-Christian World: A Selection of Essays* (Grand Rapids: William B. Eerdmans, 1969).

CHAPTER 1: SIN AS PREDATOR

1. *The Terminator*, directed by James Cameron (Orion Pictures, 1984).
2. *The Terminator*, directed by James Cameron (Orion Pictures, 1984).

3. Cornelius Plantinga Jr., *Not the Way It's Supposed to Be: A Breviary of Sin* (Grand Rapids: Eerdmans Publishing Company, 1996).

4. Frances Perkins, *The Roosevelt I Knew* (New York: Penguin Publishing Group, 2011), 148.

5. C. S. Lewis, *Mere Christianity* (New York: HarperOne, 2001), 131–32.

6. Plantinga, *Not the Way It's Supposed to Be*, 69.

CHAPTER 2: SIN AS SELF-DECEPTION

1. William Shakespeare, "King Henry the Fifth, Act IV, Scene III, lines 80–125," in *The Complete Works of William Shakespeare* (New York: Barnes & Noble, 2015), 503–6.

2. "Documenting History: Eisenhower and the Holocaust (U.S. National Park Service)," accessed February 27, 2025, https://www.nps.gov /articles/000/eisenhower-and-the-holocaust.htm; Connie Gentry, "What We Fought Against: Ohrdruf," The National WWII Museum, New Orleans, April 4, 2020, https://www.nationalww2museum.org /war/articles/ohrdruf-concentration-camp.

3. Elisabeth Elliot, "The Glory of God's Will," *Elisabeth Elliot*, May 1, 1976, https://elisabethelliot.org/resource-library/lectures -talks/the-glory-of-gods-will/.

CHAPTER 3: SIN AS LEAVEN

1. *The English Poems of George Herbert*, ed. Helen Wilcox (Cambridge University Press, 2007), 661.

2. John Owen, *Mortification of Sin* (United States: Reformed Church Publications, 2015), 19.

CHAPTER 4: SIN AS MISTRUST

1. One version of the encounter is quoted in the *Tampa Bay Times*: Thomas Churchill Dunn, "Churchill's Humorous Retorts Are Memorable," *Tampa Bay Times*, October 9, 2005, https://www .tampabay.com/archive/1993/09/16/churchill-s-humorous -retorts-are-memorable/.

2. Cynthia Heimel, "The Celebrity Decade," Tongue in Chic, *The Village Voice*, January 2, 1990.

NOTES

CHAPTER 5: SIN AS SELF-RIGHTEOUSNESS

1. George Whitefield, "The Method of Grace," *Blue Letter Bible*, accessed January 29, 2025, https://www.blueletterbible.org /study/he_is_risen/george_whitefield/witf_058.cfm.
2. *Chariots of Fire*, directed by Hugh Hudson (United Kingdom: Allied Stars, 1981).

CHAPTER 7: SIN AS LEPROSY (PART 2)

1. Rebecca Manley Pippert, *Hope Has Its Reasons: The Search to Satisfy Our Deepest Longings* (Downers Grove, IL: InterVarsity Press, 2001), 118–19.
2. C. S. Lewis, *Surprised by Joy: The Shape of My Early Life* (New York: Mariner, 2012), 227.
3. "To pay the price of usefulness" suggests that being useful to God often involves enduring hardship, surrendering personal desires, and cultivating a heart of humility, faith, and selflessness. In this context, the little girl paid the price of usefulness through her suffering and loss. Despite her tragic circumstances—losing her family, being enslaved, and facing a bleak future—she chose to act with faith, compassion, and courage.

CHAPTER 8: SIN AS SLAVERY

1. C. S. Lewis, *The Abolition of Man* (New York: HarperOne, 2015), 83–104.
2. Aldous Huxley, *Ends and Means: An Enquiry into the Nature of Ideals and into the Methods Employed for Their Realization* (New York: Harper & Brothers, 1937), 273.
3. Jonathan Edwards, *Sinners in the Hands of an Angry God* (Enfield, CT: 1741).
4. Proverbs 30:16: ". . . the grave, the barren womb, land, which is never satisfied with water, and fire, which never says, 'Enough!'"

CHAPTER 9: HEALING OF SIN: TRUE REPENTANCE

1. Thomas Watson, *The Doctrine of Repentance* (La Vergne, TN: Antiquarius, 2021).

CHAPTER 10: HEALING OF SIN: INTIMACY WITH GOD

1. For a beautiful examination of this principle that I believe is impossible to refute, read Jonathan Edwards's book *The Freedom of the Will*.

2. Stephen Charnock, "On God's Patience (From *The Existence and Attributes of God*)," Monergism, accessed February 13, 2025, https://www.monergism.com/gods-patience-stephen-charnock.

3. John Newton, "Looking at the Cross," The John Newton Project, accessed January 29, 2025, https://www.johnnewton.org/Articles/371426/The_John_Newton/new_menus/Hymns/OH_Book_2/OH_Book_2.aspx.

4. "Martin Luther's 95 Theses," accessed March 20, 2025, https://www.luther.de/en/95thesen.html.

5. Westminster Confession of Faith, 15.4.